The Life and Times of
Le Bronco von der Löwenhöhle

THE LIFE AND TIMES OF
Le Bronco
von der Löwenhöhle

*Stories and Tips from Thirteen Years
with a Leonberger*

Thomas Wikman

Thebes Press
DALLAS

Copyright © 2022 by Thomas Wikman

All rights reserved

This book is the exclusive intellectual property of the author. The text may be quoted for the purposes of marketing, promotion, and reviews. Any other use of the material herein, including for classroom instruction, workshops, readings, and other events, requires the permission of the author and/or his legal representatives. Thank you for respecting authors' rights.

Photographs on pages 7 and 80 by Aaron Brothers
Photograph on page 106 (left) © Shutterstock/Holly Kuchera
Image on page 132 courtesy of Wikimedia Commons: DEU Leonberg Böblingen
  COA.svg/Artist: Chris die Seele
Photograph on page 190 © Shutterstock/Eric Isselee

ISBN: 978-0-9980849-5-4
E-book ISBN: 978-0-9980849-6-1

Drawings by Naomi Rosenblatt
Book design by Susan Hood Design

Manufactured in the United States of America

This book is dedicated to the memory of

LE BRONCO VON DER LÖWENHÖHLE

and to the dogs he grew up with—
Baylor, Baby, Ryu, Daisy, and Rollo

CONTENTS

Preface		ix
Chapter 1	"Let's Do Le Bronco von der Löwenhöhle"	1
Chapter 2	Bronco the Very Big Dog	9
Chapter 3	Adventures at Home	20
Chapter 4	Baylor and Baby	30
Chapter 5	Ryu and Daisy	43
Chapter 6	Adventures in the Backyard and Beyond	56
Chapter 7	Adventures in the Backyard and Beyond Part II	65
Intermezzo	Baylor and Baby Pass	73
Chapter 8	Gustatory and Other Perils	81
Intermezzo	Ryu Passes	97
Chapter 9	Rollo Rolls In	100
Chapter 10	Black October and the Grey Muzzle Award	114
Intermezzo	The Last Car Ride	125
Chapter 11	History of the Leonberger	131

Chapter 12 Getting a Leonberger	143
Chapter 13 Leonberger Health	160
Acknowledgments	181
Appendix 1 The Leonberger Breed Standard	183
Appendix 2 The Worldwide Independent Leonberger Database	192
Appendix 3 Leonberger Quiz	195
Resources and References	199

PREFACE

This book is a biography of the amazing, brave, beautiful, loyal, and loving Leonberger Bronco, who came to live with me and my family—my wife, Claudia; our sons, Jacob and David; and our daughter, Rachel—in 2007. He was our best friend and a big presence in our lives. He lived an unusually long time for a Leonberger, and he left us a long list of stories to tell—funny moments, crazy adventures, and tales of his larger-than-life personality. It is when everyday life is interrupted by the unexpected that you really experience what it means to own a dog, and Leonbergers are full of surprises.

This book also tells the stories of the dogs Bronco grew up with. When he came into our household, we already had a Labrador retriever mix, Baylor, and a German shepherd, Baby. When Bronco was around a year old, we got Ryu, a Japanese Chin, then almost a year later, Daisy, a pug. Much later, when Bronco was eleven years old, we would get Rollo, a miniature Australian shepherd. Bronco's love for and tolerance of his dog siblings was truly amazing to see. He protected them, played with them, saved their lives, shared his food with them, and wanted to be with them all the time. They were his family, and he felt responsible for their safety and care.

In addition, this book is an introduction to the Leonberger breed—its history, standards, care, training, and health. I will discuss the cost of owning a Leonberger, where to get one, and whether a Leonberger is the right dog for you. This information is provided for non-experts: it's basic, but I hope it will prove helpful to Leonberger owners and prospective Leonberger owners.

Leonbergers are gentle giants. They are confident, brave, insensitive to noise, good with children and other dogs, and very social. They are family dogs and loyal companions. They are also big, powerful, full of energy, and can be rambunctious when they're young. Also, unfortunately, Leonbergers usually do not live very long—on average, eight years. Still, Bronco lived to be almost thirteen.

We got Bronco as a fourteenth birthday present for our son Jacob. But Bronco wasn't just any birthday present. Getting a Leonberger is an affair that is much bigger than simply buying a gift. We had researched the breed; we knew that Leonbergers require a lot of exercise, training, brushing, attention, and space. We knew that Leonbergers are big and strong and expensive to care for. Raising a Leonberger is a commitment that not everyone is capable of making. In fact our breeder made sure that we were fit to be Leonberger owners before she would sell us one.

We were not perfect Leonberger owners by any means, though. We learned along the way. So don't get too hung up about the mismatches between the information and advice I provide and our own lack of perfection. Instead, laugh at us—I mean, with us—learn from our mistakes, and strive to be better dog parents than we were. Most of all, I invite you to continue reading and discover how eventful, fun, and fulfilling the experience of Leonberger ownership can be.

CHAPTER 1

"Let's Do Le Bronco von der Löwenhöhle"

It was a quiet evening, and I was home alone. My wife, Claudia, was visiting her parents a few blocks away with Rachel, our daughter. Our son Jacob was meeting with his debate team; our other son, David, was visiting a friend.

I was making myself a ham sandwich in the kitchen when I suddenly felt a hand on my right shoulder. I startled and turned my head to face what I feared was an intruder, and there he stood on his hind legs—our Leonberger, Bronco. His big paw on my shoulder felt for a moment exactly like a human hand.

Bronco looked at me with his kind, wise eyes, then he looked at the sandwich. Then he turned his head toward me again and held my gaze. At that moment I understood what he wanted. I cut the sandwich in two and gave him his half.

I should explain that we had a problem with a trespasser at that time, which was the reason I was startled. This trespasser would sit outside our bedroom window at night and make threats and shout obscene comments at Claudia when I was not present. At first, though, we didn't know where the threats and comments were coming from. I doubted Claudia's accounts of these incidents, especially because she thought the voice might be coming from within our bedroom, perhaps via an electronic speaker. I thought she was just having nightmares.

Then one night I heard it myself—a voice screaming, "I am going to burn your house down!" Just as Claudia had said, it sounded like it came from within our bedroom, almost as if it were right next to me.

After Claudia and I went through our "Oh, so now you believe me" routine, I started looking under our bed and inside the heating and air-conditioning vents for hidden speakers and/or microphones. It was hard to believe that someone had planted these things in our bedroom, but that seemed to be the case.

Then it finally dawned on me. Next to the headboard of our bed, on Claudia's side, just inches from her pillow, is a window. At night, when the blinds are lowered and the slats are partially open, you can see in, even if we have just a few lights on in the house. But of course under these conditions, you can't see anything that might be outside.

I ran out the front door and around the back of the house, and there, right in front of our bedroom window, was one of our lawn chairs. The trespasser had climbed our fence, taken the chair, sat down in front of the window, and spied on us. Whenever I left the room, he would shout obscenities and threats at Claudia. When his face was planted in front of our window, he was just two or three feet away. This was why the voice felt so close. This had been going on for two weeks. We were happy to have finally figured it out, but we realized we had a problem.

We talked to our neighbors about the situation, and they told us that the trespasser had terrorized them as well. He had been quite busy looking through bedroom windows at night. People in the

neighborhood were scared. I called the police, who told us they could do nothing unless the man was caught in the act or he committed a crime other than trespassing.

Therefore, I decided to hire private investigators. I found them in the phone book. Phone books still existed back then.

The investigators told me that they typically spy on people suspected of cheating on their spouses, so this would be a more interesting job for them. The plan was for them to hide behind the bushes in our backyard and in a dark car parked on our street. When the man appeared, they would record him on video. They had a lot of fancy equipment and instruments, including big microphones, cameras, and metal detectors. They reminded us of Ghostbusters with all their technology and enthusiasm. They clearly loved their job. Unfortunately, though, the trespasser didn't show up, so after a couple of days I decided to let the investigators go.

However, I soon figured out who the trespasser was. I started paying attention to what was going on in the neighborhood, and one evening, I noticed a strange-looking but relatively young man, apparently homeless, who seemed to be stealthily roaming our neighborhood. I did not confront him, because I had no proof.

But a few days later, I heard shuffling noises outside our bedroom window. The trespasser was finally back. This time I sent Bronco out to chase him, and he did. Like the detectives, Bronco was enthusiastic but didn't catch him. Still, he chased the man off. Having a big bearlike dog rushing toward you at night is probably a bit unnerving, even if the dog just wants to lick you. We never experienced or heard about the problem after this event, so Bronco may have helped the entire neighborhood.

A couple of weeks later, while walking Bronco on a neighboring block, I saw the homeless man across the street, at a bit of a distance. He stared at us in fright. Bronco just calmly looked at him without barking. The man was clearly terrified of Bronco, and he ran away.

But despite the nightmare the homeless man had inflicted on us, I felt sorry for him. My guess is that he was suffering from mental illness and that he had had a very tough and lonely life.

What's in a Name?

You may have figured out from the title of this book and the title of this chapter that Bronco's full name was Le Bronco von der Löwenhöhle. However, his name on the original pedigree certificate from the Leonberger Club of America was even more interesting: "Lets do le Bronco von der Löwenhöhle"—yes, without the apostrophe. How did that happen?

The Leonberger is a noble and relatively rare breed, and purebred Leonbergers typically have a long pedigree that can be traced back to the beginning of the twentieth century. This means that if you buy one, you and your dog will become part of a special community, and your dog's name will reflect that. Bronco's last name, von der Löwenhöhle, means that he originated from Kennel von der Löwenhöhle.

During an email exchange with the person writing up Bronco's pedigree certificate, we were informed that because our dog was born in a litter identified by the letter *L*, his official name needed to begin with an *L*, too, even though at home we could call our dog whatever we liked. We knew we wanted to name him Bronco, which we thought was appropriate for a Leonberger, so later Claudia wrote, "Let's do Le Bronco," intending that the dog's name would begin with the word "Le," fulfilling the kennel's requirement.

But when we received a copy of Bronco's pedigree, we saw that our correspondent had misunderstood and included the words "Let's do" as part of the name! Well, "Let's do" starts with an *L*, too, so it fulfilled the pedigree requirement. And that's how Bronco's official full name came to be Lets do le Bronco von der Löwenhöhle.

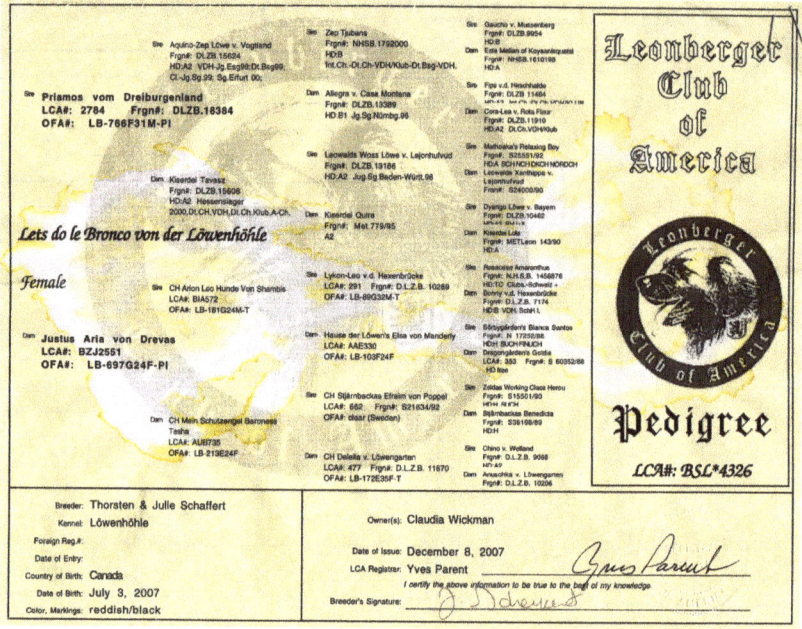

We were surprised to see Bronco's official name as it appeared on his pedigree.

There were other mistakes on the certificate, too: Bronco was classified as female, and our last name was misspelled as Wickman. We later got these mistakes corrected in the Worldwide Independent Leonberger Database, and some mistakes were corrected on the registration certificate from the American Kennel Club, which we got in 2010, after the Leonberger was recognized by the AKC. But none of that mattered much to us: we knew his name; Jacob knew his name; Bronco knew his name. Plus, we got a good story out of it.

A Dramatic Arrival

Kennel von der Löwenhöhle is located in Vancouver, Canada, and we live in Dallas. So even though the owners do not normally do this,

"Let's Do Le Bronco von der Löwenhöhle"

they agreed to have Bronco shipped to us by air. He was between nine and ten weeks old at the time.

On the appointed day, the plane from Seattle arrived late. Claudia and I drove to the Dallas airport to pick him up. At the designated arrivals gate, we asked about Bronco and were told that we were at the wrong place—pets are picked up at a special cargo location. The

This photo of Bronco was taken when he was around three months old, soon after we got him.

airline employees explained to us how to get there and told us that the cargo location was closing at 11:00 p.m., only a few minutes away.

We felt stupid. Why didn't we find this out beforehand? Poor Bronco had endured a long plane trip in a crate, and now his new parents might not be there to pick him up. How would he feel if he had to stay overnight alone in a crate in a cargo hall? He was a young puppy, and he didn't know what was going on.

We ran to the parking garage, searched for our car, and found it pretty quickly. People must have wondered what we were running from as we dashed out of the terminal. We drove out of the garage James Bond style—fast, but not so fast that we would risk having an accident. (I'm pretty good at driving fast and safely at the same time, but it doesn't happen often—I promise.) We followed the directions we had been given, making sure we did not miss any turns or exits. Our stress levels were maxed out, and our hearts were pumping. Fortunately, we arrived at the cargo building at 10:55 p.m. and were very relieved when the attendants let us in. We ran to the counter and asked for Bronco. And there they had him.

Bronco was the cutest puppy in the world. He looked like a brown bear cub. He didn't know us, yet he was so happy to see us. He was full of life. We could smell that he had peed on himself in his crate. He didn't seem to care, so we didn't care. We held him in our arms and kissed him. As soon as we came home, we washed him and gave him something to eat and drink. We introduced him to our other two dogs—Baylor, a Labrador retriever mix, and Baby, a German shepherd. They were older dogs whom we had gotten from relatives who in turn had gotten them from shelters.

Early the next morning, we placed Bronco next to our soon-to-be-fourteen-year-old son, and when he woke up, he found a fed, clean, and happy Leonberger puppy next to him. Happiness was in our house.

CHAPTER 2

Bronco the Very Big Dog

Bronco was a big dog. As an adult, when he was not overweight, he tipped the scales at 135 pounds. He was significantly bigger than a German shepherd, and when he stood on his hind legs, he could easily put his big paws on a person's shoulders, even if that person was almost six feet tall. Naturally, his size, combined with his energetic nature, made him a perfect dance partner, and Bronco loved dancing. His size and energy also combined to produce a lot of good stories.

When Bronco arrived at our house from the airport, for example, we had prepared a very large crate for him to sleep in. Unfortunately, even though it was spacious, he didn't like it very much. As time went on, he decided that he wanted to abandon the crate and sleep with us in our bed. It was difficult to say no and listen to him whine at night. So Claudia lay down on the floor next to him and put her hand into the crate and petted him and held his paw. He loved that and was able to fall asleep that way.

Eventually, though, we relented and let him sleep in our bed. As the saying goes, "First they take your heart, then your bed." But as Bronco quickly grew to 120 pounds, and then to 130 pounds, that arrangement didn't work very well. We were three in the bed, and Bronco would sleep between us, a situation that became a bit crowded. Sometimes Bronco would push me with his paws until I fell off the bed and onto the floor. To my great relief, as time passed, he started to prefer the dog mattresses that we bought for him.

On the other hand, Bronco was relatively easy to potty train. He quickly learned to go number two outside, but the peeing outside took a little longer, so Claudia hired a trainer from our veterinarian's office to help us out. As a result, Bronco was mostly potty trained by four months old.

I was often working long hours, and Claudia was at home with our

Irun

When Claudia was a child, one of her favorite dogs was a German shepherd named Irun. One day, when the family was living in Akron, Ohio, Irun escaped and was captured by the local dogcatcher. Claudia's mother was summoned to court, and Claudia, who was around eleven years old at the time, came with her. Claudia loved Irun and was worried about what the judge would do, especially to Irun, so she told him, "Judge, I know where you live"—and she did. Fortunately, Claudia's mother got off with just a fine.

kids, so it was she who mostly took care of Bronco, especially in the early years. She took him for walks every morning; she took him to the dog park, to go shopping, to Starbucks, and other places. She socialized him well. She also brushed him a few times a week, kept him clean, gave him medication to prevent heartworm and repel fleas and ticks,* and took him to the veterinarian's office and the groomer. All of us in the family helped with the training, but Claudia did most of it. She grew up with dogs, so she knew what she was doing, and she did a very good job.

Walking and the Boy Who Cried Wolf

Bronco was eager to learn, and he liked to go for walks, but he didn't always finish them. When he got tired, he lifted his front paws up and scratched our legs. Then we picked him up and carried him. He loved being carried around like a baby. We carried him when he was thirty pounds and when he was fifty pounds, but at one hundred pounds it was time to stop.

Walking a big strong dog like Bronco presents special challenges. You need to be physically fit in order to control a Leonberger who isn't listening to you. On several occasions Bronco yanked the leash so hard when I walked him that I almost fell forward. Did I mention that it's not a good idea to wear flip-flops while you're walking a big strong dog? When our daughter, Rachel, did, she fell face-first after Bronco got excited and took off in pursuit of something. She shouted at him to come back, and he did. I guess he felt bad for her and returned. That was his personality.

One time, when Claudia was walking Bronco at White Rock Lake

---

* This medication also protects against infestations of chewing lice: see "Dog Lice: What They Are, How to Avoid Them," American Kennel Club, June 24, 2020, at https://www.akc.org/expert-advice/health/can-dogs-get-lice/.

Park, just outside Dallas, Bronco saw a dog whom, for whatever reason, he did not like. He started running toward the dog and its owner. Claudia, taken by surprise, had a hard time controlling the situation. Bronco pulled her along as she tried to keep her balance. The man with the other dog saw that a potential confrontation was developing, and he loudly screamed, "Noooooo," at Bronco. Then Bronco just stopped. He understood, and it all ended well.

It was incidents like these that prompted us to hire a professional dog trainer from Bark Busters and buy a Gentle Leader harness, which has a loop that fits around your dog's nose. When your dog pulls forward, the motion gently moves his head to the side, redirecting his attention back to you. It may be a little bit uncomfortable for the dog, but it is certainly infinitely better than a shock collar, which is something you should never use.

One day I was standing in our living room, talking to the Bark Busters trainer. Bronco was standing behind me, and he kept poking my leg with his paw. I ignored him because I was in the middle of a conversation. Suddenly Bronco bit me on the rear end. It was not an aggressive bite, but it was a big one, and it hurt. He could easily have bitten me much harder, of course.

I turned around, and there stood Bronco, looking at me with his happy eyes and wagging his tail as if he were completely innocent. I forgave him instantly.

I asked the trainer, "Why did he do that?"

She said, "He was trying to get your attention, but you were ignoring him, so he bit you." She continued, "He should know that he is not the one in charge, and he shouldn't do that." She knew what she was talking about. I should add that this was the only time Bronco bit anyone.

Once when I was walking Bronco around the neighborhood, a neighbor who always let his black Labs run loose saw us. He shouted to his wife, "Honey, get the dogs inside! Someone is walking a bear out here." I guess letting your large dogs run loose isn't a problem until someone walks a dog much bigger than yours.

On a number of occasions, we've met people who said to us that Bronco is the biggest dog they've ever seen. However, there are bigger dogs. We've met bigger English bullmastiffs and bigger Great Danes.

One day I took Bronco into PetSmart, and after I did my shopping, he and I were standing in the checkout line. Bronco was very quiet and well behaved, but a boy ahead of us in line became quite alarmed when he saw us. He shouted, "Look! A wolf, a wolf, a wolf!" He pointed his finger at Bronco. His mom tried to calm the boy, but he would not stop shouting. He didn't seem to be afraid of Bronco, but he was really concerned that there was a big wolf in the pet store. I tried to explain to the boy that Bronco was not a wolf. He was just a big dog.

Bronco was not only big, he was also confident and unafraid and insensitive to noise. Most dogs I've known have been afraid of lightning and thunder and loud explosions, but not Bronco. Here in Texas, thunderstorms can be very violent and dangerous. North Texas is located in Tornado Alley, and that's where the world's worst thunderstorms occur. We've had our share of lightning strikes, heavy rain, flooded streets, sixty-mile-an-hour winds, giant hail, and tornadoes. You don't want to be outside when a severe thunderstorm is at hand.

Once when I was out walking Bronco, we were surprised by one of those Tornado Alley–style supercell thunderstorms, and lightning struck the ground maybe one hundred yards away from us. It was bright, but above all the following thunderclap was very loud. It was an explosion more than anything else. I jumped where I stood, and my heart was pounding afterward. Bronco, on the other hand, was too busy sniffing something interesting to pay attention to the sound. After the lightning strike, he looked up as if to make sure everything was okay, then he continued with his important olfactory project. I can assure you that he was not deaf. My repeated failure to quietly open a cheese wrapper in the kitchen without his noticing is proof of that.

Bronco the "People Person"

Leonbergers love to give hugs. They don't do it by wrapping their arms around us, and neither do they understand what it means when we humans wrap our arms around them, which they can interpret as a kind of restraint. Instead, a Leonberger hug is given when the dog leans on you and snuggles his head or chest against you. Bronco loved doing that. He was a very loving dog. But even though Leonberger hugs are sweet, they can be a problem for the elderly and short people. This was something we had to watch out for. However, if you can handle a Leonberger hug, it is one of the most wonderful things you can experience.

When Bronco was young, our daughter, Rachel, was on the school soccer team. We brought Bronco to the games, and her team chose him as a mascot. The girls loved him. At halftime, and before and after games, they would stand in line to pet him. Even the opposing team wanted to pet him. You may think that having dozens of girls petting him would be too much for Bronco, but it wasn't. He loved every minute of it.

The Joys of Walking

Taking dogs for a walk can be fun for you as well as for them if you pay attention. It's a time for experience as well as exercise. You meet people and other dogs; you'll see children playing; you'll pass joggers, bicyclists, mopeds, and other animals—cats, rabbits, squirrels, ducks, geese, opossums, frogs, lizards, and foxes. The sky may be blue; it might be windy, sunny, or cloudy; there are trees, bushes, flowers, grass, and houses of all colors and sizes, some quite interesting to look at. There are sounds and sights, things to touch—but above all, there are so many smells. Dogs like to smell and sniff everything, and you should let them. Walking dogs is a beautiful experience. Learn from them, and you'll be happier for it. The neighborhood can be a wonderful world.

I often find myself amazed by how keenly perceptive and curious dogs are. Sometimes when Bronco saw a squirrel, he would watch it intently until it disappeared up a tree. Then he would turn around and look at me as if asking, "Where did it go?" I would point to the squirrel up in the tree, and he would look to the place where I was pointing, seeming to say, "Oh, never mind." Then we would continue walking.

Speech, reading, mathematics, written communication—these are the superpowers of the human animal. They allow us to know things that dogs don't know. But smelling things that are beyond a human's ability to sense is one of *dogs'* superpowers. It allows them to know things that we don't know. That's why it's important to let dogs explore the world through their noses. You need to let them sniff.

Bronco was an extremely affectionate dog.

At first the coach approved of it. Bronco's presence made the soccer games more interesting. However, after a while he felt that the girls were paying too much attention to Bronco and too little attention to the game. He asked us if we perhaps would consider leaving him at home sometimes. We didn't want to do that, so we came up with alternatives, such as walking him nearby.

Bronco also loved trick-or-treating on Halloween. He enjoyed being with the children and going from house to house, and our kids were proud to have their big dog along. We should have dressed him up—it would have been fun—but we didn't. He looked like a lion anyway. Naturally, he couldn't eat the candy, but he got a doggie-appropriate treat when we got home. He was never afraid of any of the costumes or props. The only thing that seemed to bother him was the scarecrow that we had on our front lawn. He barked incessantly at that scarecrow every time we walked outside.

Like any dog, Bronco loved greeting people. He ran to the door very excitedly whenever someone came over. Unfortunately, in the beginning he would jump up on people. He would put his paws on their shoulders or, worse, bump his nose into their noses. We eventually got him to stop doing this, but nevertheless we got some funny stories out of it. Of course we didn't intentionally allow funny things to happen. We really tried to solve Bronco's behavior issues, but it doesn't hurt to tell the stories after the fact.

For example, when Bronco was young, we used to have windows on either side of our front door. The windows were placed around five feet up from the floor so that you could look out and in, assuming you were not too short. (We would later replace our front door and windows with something that felt more secure.) Back then, mail carriers and people delivering packages could look through these windows to see if we were home. It also meant that Bronco could easily look out the window himself if he stood on his hind legs.

One day, a UPS deliveryman rang our doorbell, and when no one answered, he placed his face at the window and shaded his eyes to see if anyone was home. That's when Bronco's big happy face slammed into the window from the other side. It was a sudden face-to-face encounter, complete with a big tongue. The UPS guy jumped backwards from the surprise. Then we opened the door and accepted the package. The man was somewhat shaken, but he was fine.

On another occasion, one of our neighbors came over to say hello to our new puppy. We'd had Bronco for almost a year by then, so he was big. As our neighbor entered our hallway, Bronco came running, and before I had a chance to stop him, he jumped up and put his paws on our neighbor's shoulders. This man is somewhat short, so Bronco was able to lick his head, which he proceeded to do. Then

Bronco did something we were totally unprepared for. You know the circus trick in which the lion tamer puts his head in the lion's mouth? Yes, that's the trick Bronco performed on our friendly neighbor.

Bronco was just playing and having fun, but that's not how to greet a neighbor. I apologized profusely, but our neighbor said that it was perfectly all right and that there was no harm done. He looked a bit

> ### No Jumping!
>
> Leonberger puppies jump up on you and on visitors. But dogs jumping up on people is never a good thing. A little dog jumping up and touching the knee of a visitor may not be a big deal. In fact, some people think it's sort of cute. However, with Leonbergers this problem is bigger—much bigger. A Leonberger jumping up on a neighbor and trying to swallow his head is embarrassing. A Leonberger jumping up on Grandma and making her fall and break her hip is a major disaster.
>
> Leonbergers love jumping up on children, too, because they're small, and this may frighten them. The children may even get hurt. Jumping up on people is something every Leonberger owner should be prepared to deal with.
>
> One thing you can do is turn your back as soon as your puppy jumps on you. You can also put the dog on a leash and gently but firmly tug on it when he jumps. Removing him from the room for a while—giving him a time-out—may also discourage him from jumping. One thing that worked very well for us is filling a spray bottle with water and spraying it on the puppy when he jumps. We found that plain water was good enough. The surprise will deter him from jumping again (eventually).

unnerved, and obviously he had not expected to be part of a circus act, but he said that Bronco was a wonderful dog and that he really loved the big galoot.

Despite what happened, our neighbor was always very nice to Bronco. However, for us that first encounter was a red flag. We had to get the jumping-up-on-people problem under control.

CHAPTER 3

Adventures at Home

You shouldn't leave a Leonberger home alone for a long period of time, and for the most part we didn't, but it happened sometimes that we had to go out and leave him for a few hours. As we found out, however, Leonbergers can accomplish a lot in the interim.

One day when I came home from work and Claudia was not at home, I saw that the sofas, chairs, and tables had been moved around. I assumed it was Claudia who had done this. I was thinking, slightly annoyed, "She's never happy with the way the house looks. She always has to change things." Then I moved the furniture back to where it had been.

The next day, the same thing happened, but this time I discovered the truth. As I walked in the door, Bronco was in the process of dragging a sofa across the living room. He clamped his jaws onto one of the legs, then little by little he tugged it across the length of the room before moving on to the next piece of furniture. The sofa was pretty heavy; I had a hard time moving it by myself. It was he, not Claudia, who was determined to give the house a new look.

Because of this incident and others—including the time he chewed our wedding album—we decided to buy and install pet gates to restrict his movements. They needed to be sturdy, so we bought the kind that were made of metal. We nailed some of them to the walls and had professionals install the others. Bronco still had ample space and was free to roam the house when someone was at home. But when we left for a dinner engagement or some other obligation, we closed the gates. Amazingly, however, Bronco learned how to lift the latches with his nose and then push the gates open with his paw. So to prevent future breakouts, we had to lock them in place. Bronco was not only very big, he was also very smart.

The Eye Drop War

One day we noticed that Bronco's eyes were red, so we took him to the veterinarian. He was around one year old at the time. The veterinarian told us that Bronco had conjunctivitis and that all we needed to do was give him eye drops. But giving a very big dog eye drops turned out to be a lot more challenging than we had anticipated. "Just give him three drops two times a day"—easy peasy, right? Well, the veterinarian might as well have told us to wrestle a bear on a tightrope while juggling.

Whenever we approached Bronco with the eyedropper, he ran off. Almost nothing else scared him—thunder and lightning, explosions, large hail, other big dogs, noisy crowds—but he was terrified of eye drops. Once we would catch up with him, he would thwart any attempt on our part to put the drops in. He would jump up and down while violently shaking his head back and forth and closing his eyes. So Claudia and I and Jacob and David decided we needed to do it all together.

We made what we thought was a great plan: two people were going to hold Bronco down on the floor while keeping his head still. A third person would hold his eyelids open, and a fourth person would put in the eye drops, being careful not to touch his eyes in the process. Poor Bronco was certainly not going to like it, but what else could we do? He needed his medicine.

We chased Bronco around the house and finally caught him in the living room. He struggled, but we were able to hold him down. However, before we could open his eyelids, he made a sudden and powerful move that got all five of us rolling like a giant snowball into the metal pet gate that stood between the family room and the living room. With a loud bang, we crashed into the gate. The screws that fastened it to the wall popped out and shot across the room. We had turned into a messy dog-and-people pile on the floor.

Bronco was the first one to get up. As he stood and surveyed the carnage, we acknowledged our defeat. Claudia put away the eye drops. I put the pet gate in the garage. No more eye drops; no more pet gate; no more forcing anything on Bronco. He had been victorious in the Eye Drop War, and he knew it.

As it happened, the conjunctivitis healed without the drops. We

---

Food—The Great Motivator

Pray that you don't have to give your Leonberger eye drops, but if you do, first ask your veterinarian for instructions. If those don't work, take a step-by-step approach: give the dog a treat for standing still, then a treat for letting you hold his head, then a treat for allowing the drops in his eyes. You can also warm the drops in your pocket so they don't feel cold.*

* For other helpful tips, see Videojug, "How to Apply Dog Eye Drops," at https://www.youtube.com/watch?v=O3awEUJmK8o, uploaded April 12, 2011.

would later learn that it *is* possible to get eye drops into a Leonberger's eyes without going to war.

It's Called *Fur*-niture for a Reason

Something you have to be prepared for if you visit our house is that we let our dogs sit and sleep on our sofas, chairs, and beds. So if one of our dogs wants to sit on the sofa, please move over and give him room. There might be some dog hair on your clothing, but you can brush it off.

One of our sofas is actually too big to sit comfortably on. It is wide

This sofa was too big for people, but not too big for Bronco.

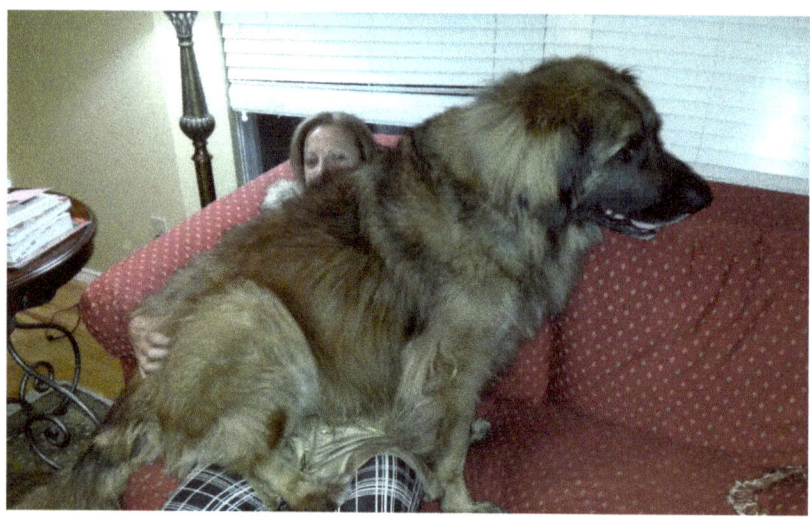

Claudia is dwarfed by a 167-pound "lapdog."

in all directions, and you have to lean really far back when you sit on it. However, Bronco loved this sofa.

Unlike his small dog siblings, Bronco could not sit in our laps easily. He tried, though, as you can see in the photo above. Of course, at the time this picture was taken, Bronco was overweight—167 pounds. We knew we shouldn't have allowed him to gain that much weight, and shortly thereafter, we put him on a diet. He was on that diet for a while, and he was not happy. I guess most of us aren't happy when we're on a diet. In any case, 167 pounds in Claudia's lap was a tad much. Poor Bronco and poor Claudia.

Bronco's Hamster Search and Rescue

Back when Bronco was young, the kids had pet hamsters—Moldova and Montenegro. The hamsters escaped from their cages sometimes, but Bronco usually helped us find them whenever they did. Claudia would tell him, "Bronco, find the hamsters," and he would go around the house sniffing until he found them. One time he found them in the linen closet; another time he found them on a shelf in the living room.

On one occasion, a friend of David trusted us with his two hamsters while he and his family went on vacation. A couple of days later, Claudia noticed that the two hamsters were missing from their cage. The next thing she noticed was that Bronco's cheeks looked puffy, so she said, "Bronco, drop it!" Out came the two hamsters, both unconscious.

In a panic, Claudia started performing CPR on the unconscious hamsters. She put one hamster at a time in her hand and gently compressed each tiny chest using the finger of the other hand. Fortunately, one hamster revived right away. The CPR didn't seem to be working on the other hamster, but Claudia put both of them back in their cage, and soon the second hamster also woke up. We decided to keep the incident to ourselves. Hamsters don't squeal.

The question is, Did Bronco try to eat the hamsters? Or did he

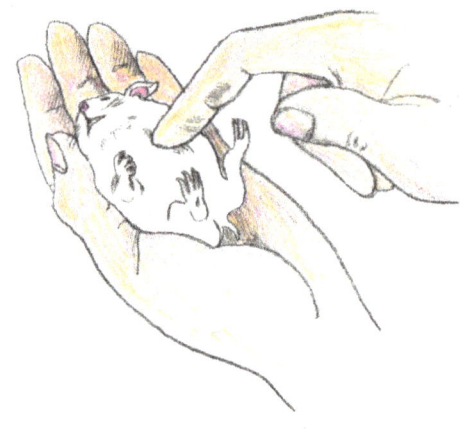

The Dog of My Dreams

I dreamed about Bronco and tornadoes years before our neighborhood was ravaged, for real, by an EF3 tornado, in October of 2019. In my dream, Claudia and the children were inside a baseball stadium while I was walking Bronco outside. Then tornadoes started to appear, and he and I ran to the stadium to warn the spectators and find Claudia and the children. However, once we got inside the stadium, we saw that it was empty. It turned out that everyone was already in a tornado shelter. Then a tornado hit the stadium and destroyed most of it. At that point, Bronco and I ran away as fast as we could. We hid in some ditches.

Bronco seemed nervous, so I spoke to him soothingly. That's when I saw a log cabin standing not far off. We ran to it and took shelter inside. Unfortunately, a tornado appeared and lifted the cabin high in the air. After a tumultuous ride, it landed softly on the ground. I turned around and said to Bronco, "That wasn't so bad, was it?"

simply find them and pick them up, intending to alert us to their presence? I've asked several people this question, including some who know Leonbergers well. The answer they give is that he tried to save them from whatever danger he thought they might have been in. If he wanted to eat them, they say, he would have tried chewing them. But clearly, he didn't.

The hamsters may have felt differently about the situation and may have fainted from the shock. Who knows? Bronco was a hero on many occasions, but this time, perhaps, he was a hamster superhero.

Eventually our own hamsters died, but that didn't end Bronco's

---

Then I had a dream in which Bronco was transformed into a lion. I was driving my Prius, and all of a sudden Bronco turned into a lion while he was sitting in the back seat. His head grew, and he placed his big lion head between the front seats and settled it on the armrest between them. He looked out the front window, the way he does in real life. Then we saw a terrible car accident. We stopped, and I took Bronco outside so that together we could help the victims. Bronco was very kind and wanted to help, but everyone was frightened of the lion, so we gave up and left.

On another occasion, I dreamed that we painted Bronco with stripes and put a tiger mask over his face. Then a female white tiger showed up and started following Bronco around everywhere. Ultimately, she became his companion. Claudia and I and the children weren't too happy about this because we were afraid of the tiger. But we calmed down after seeing how gentle she was with Bronco and us.

Any dream interpreters out there?

interest in them. When the first hamster died, we held a funeral. We put the hamster in a shoe box, said goodbye, put some flowers in the box, and buried it in the backyard underneath some bushes. But when we turned our backs, Bronco was there, digging under the bushes. Perhaps he thought he could save the hamster. So we called Bronco off and tried again: this time I dug a deeper hole and put a wide rock over the shoe box before covering it. Now Bronco couldn't dig up the hamster. When the second hamster died, I had learned my lesson and did the same thing.

The Day Bronco Stumped the Geek Squad

At around the time the hamsters died, the kids had a laptop that they used for playing games and—allegedly—doing homework. One evening, when the laptop was folded flat on a table, Bronco calmly walked over to it and bit it, as if he were taking a bite out of a sandwich. He bit it very hard—so hard that his teeth punctured the metal top and the edges curled up on each side. The force of his bite made a loud cracking sound.

The boys and I stared in amazement. The laptop looked like it had been hit with a toothed sledgehammer. It really demonstrated the immense power of Bronco's jaws. The bite force of a Leonberger has been measured at 399 PSI (pounds per square inch), which is significantly more than those of an American pit bull terrier (235 PSI), a German shepherd (238 PSI), and a Rottweiler (328 PSI).* We don't know why Bronco bit the laptop. Maybe he didn't like the computer because of all the attention it got. Thank goodness we had an extended warranty from Best Buy.

---

* Comparison List, "Dogs Bite Force Comparison," at https://www.youtube.com/watch?v=5qyvg5e2690, uploaded December 26, 2020.

We took the crushed laptop with the huge bite marks back to Best Buy and asked the technician if our extended warranty covered the damage. The man looked at the laptop, puzzled. He said, "Wow—I've never seen anything like this before." He told us that we were covered under the warranty but that he was dying to know what happened. I explained to him that our very big and very strong dog bit the laptop. He said, "That's the best story I've ever heard." I guess our extended warranty covered both acts of God and acts of Dog.

CHAPTER 4

Baylor and Baby

Our first family dog was Baylor, a yellow Labrador retriever mix who allegedly was one-quarter Rhodesian ridgeback. He was a rescue dog first adopted by our niece Jessica, and then when she went to college he stayed with Claudia's parents until we finally adopted him a couple of years later. He was familiar with us, so the change was not a difficult experience for him. Naturally he was potty trained and well trained in other regards, so taking care of him was a relatively easy job.

Baylor was the dog who taught me what it means to be a dog owner. I didn't grow up with dogs, and for years I felt like dogs were annoying and somewhat unpleasant and even scary. To me, they were just barking machines. People who let their aggressive and poorly trained dogs run loose and bother people on the street and children walking to school had cemented that impression on me. A dog was something I wasn't interested in having. Hamsters and turtles seemed a lot easier to take care of, and they don't run around growling and barking at people. But there was Baylor, and I had a lot to learn.

Baylor was an energetic and fun dog. He was also very social. He

Baylor, seen here around 2005 or 2006, had a smile that would warm the coldest hearts.

loved visiting the dog park and playing with other dogs. Like Bronco, he loved swimming. He loved running, chasing balls, and playing tug-of-war.* Over the years I grew quite fond of him. I loved coming home to his enthusiastic greetings and then taking him for a walk.

On several occasions, Baylor proved to be a hero. Claudia's mother told me that once, when she was walking him along a road near her house, she fell into a deep hole in the road. There were no other people around at the time, and the hole, which wasn't covered and hadn't been roped off, was around waist high. Not being young anymore, she couldn't climb her way out. However, Baylor started pulling her.

---

* I later learned that tug-of-war is not a great game to play with dogs. It can make them aggressive.

Baylor loved to swim in Claudia's parents' pool.

She held on to his leash while he smoothly but forcefully dragged her upward. Working together, they managed to pull her out of the hole. Baylor understood how to help, and he was strong enough to do it.

Baylor could also defend himself when he needed to. One time, as he and I were walking down a long straight road in the neighborhood, I turned around and saw two dogs running out of an alleyway around half a mile behind us. Right behind them came a woman, and she was running as well. The dogs were racing toward us and barking, and the woman behind the dogs was screaming at them. It was obvious that they had snuck out of a house and were ignoring their owner. For a moment I thought that maybe we should be running as well, but I decided against it. I would not be able to outrun the dogs, even though Baylor could, and letting him loose would be a bad idea. I decided to keep calm and continue walking.

A few seconds later I turned around to look again. The dogs were coming closer. I could see their glistening teeth and their faces full of

Six Lessons for New Dog Owners

As a formerly reluctant dog owner, I learned my lessons about life with dogs the hard way. But owning Baylor proved to be one of the most transformative and rewarding experiences of my life. I went from being uninterested in dogs to someone who loves dogs and really cares for them. Below are the things I found most important to remember about my new best friend.

1. Be caring and loving toward your dog. Dogs are not machines; they're not wild squirrels in the forest. They're family. The sooner you discover that, the sooner both of you can develop an affectionate and beneficial relationship that will enrich both your lives.

2. When your dog wants to go out, let him out, no matter how lazy you feel or how sleepy you are. Cleaning up a mess on the floor is less pleasant than opening the door. (Only let your dog out off leash if you have a fenced-in area for him to walk in.) If your dog makes a mess, don't blame him—blame yourself.

3. Dogs need exercise and time to sniff around and enjoy the outdoors. Sniffing opens up an entire universe of experiences for dogs about which we know little. We need to respect these experiences. So walk the dog and let him sniff. Play with him, throw balls for him, pet him, and socialize him.

4. Listen to your dog. Dogs tell you what they want and what they need, and they're very good at nonverbal communication.

5. Wash your dog, groom him, take him to the veterinarian, and pay attention to his health and medical needs. Stay alert for signs of physical problems.

6. Don't leave food out where your dog can get it. If he eats too much food at once, he can get sick, and if he eats too much over time he'll become overweight.

rage as they charged toward us. The woman behind them was going as fast as she could, but she couldn't keep up. Both dogs were around the size of Baylor. One of them looked like a pit bull, and the other looked like a golden retriever. I braced for the worst, and Baylor and I positioned ourselves for a fight.

Then the dog who looked like a golden retriever stopped and sat down. He seemed to be less aggressive. But the pit bull came right at us as if he wanted to kill us. There was a violent clash. Baylor fought back valiantly, and he was able to control the situation, despite being on a leash. (Well, I gave him all the leeway I could.) There were loud growls and snarls and sharp white teeth snapping and biting.

The woman finally arrived. Her face was red, and she was sweating profusely. It didn't look like she was in good shape, and she had just sprinted half a mile without stopping. Breathing heavily, she grabbed her aggressive dog and apologized. I didn't respond, even though I felt sorry for her. I knew the whole thing was probably an accident, but after that experience I couldn't spare much sympathy for her. Luckily, there were no serious injuries.

Many dog owners intentionally let their dogs run loose in public, thinking they have them under perfect control, but then the dogs snap when they don't expect it and they don't know why. It probably wasn't what happened in the episode with Baylor, but instances like this serve as powerful reminders of why we have leash laws.

After it was all over, I felt proud of Baylor for defending himself so well. He was a lot stronger and feistier than I expected, yet he was a very friendly and loving Labrador.

Well... Baylor wasn't *always* friendly. There was one exception to his affability: the mailman, his only enemy. Baylor must have considered the daily act of putting mail in our mailbox a sign of aggression. Every time the mailman came, Baylor barked loudly and threateningly. Perhaps he thought he was saving us from grave potential danger.

One day while the mailman's truck was stopped in front of our mailbox, I opened the front door—I don't remember why. Like a bolt out of the blue, Baylor ran through the opening and charged the truck. I did not expect this to happen at all. The window of the truck was open, and, to my astonishment, Baylor jumped inside. I expected certain disaster to unfold before my eyes—injuries, expensive lawsuits, prison: maybe we would be banned from receiving mail ever again. This time it wasn't the pit-bull-owning woman who was ashamed: it was I.

In a panic, I dashed toward the truck. But just as fast as he had jumped into it, Baylor jumped back out. He looked confused. He slowly walked back toward me, completely calm, and I realized that there was no one in the truck. Then I saw the mailman standing at my next-door neighbor's house ringing the doorbell. Baylor hadn't noticed him, and he hadn't noticed Baylor. I quickly and carefully approached Baylor, grabbed his collar, and took him inside. No one but I had seen what had happened. No one but I knew how close we were to disaster.

I learned a lesson that day that I will never forget. I also developed an immense respect for letter carriers and the sacrifice they make every day to bring us mail.

In addition to his hatred for mailmen, Baylor had one more vice, and that was stealing food. He was always hungry, and he was pretty good at culinary theft. On one occasion, I was standing in the kitchen holding a sandwich in my hand. Suddenly the sandwich disappeared from my fingers as if it had been teleported. I didn't feel a thing—no pull, no touch, no wet nose. It just vanished. I turned around, and behind me stood Baylor, swallowing something. He looked at me, wagging his tail. Was he innocent? Did Captain Kirk beam my sandwich to another dimension? How could I be mad at him when I didn't have proof?

On another occasion, Baylor jumped up on top of the kitchen table using a chair as a step stool and cleared it of the desserts that Claudia's grandmother had brought for the kids and the family. That's how I learned that she had a swear-word vocabulary—and that it was substantial. Fortunately, the kids weren't nearby. On yet another occasion, Baylor emptied a tray of baklava that had been sitting on the kitchen counter.

His most notable food raid was probably when he stole the Thanksgiving turkey and ran off with it. We salvaged most of it, but knowing that Baylor had been all over it, we decided not to eat what he left us. It wasn't very appetizing.

Perhaps the most annoying incident involved his theft of a pizza from the hands of our younger son, David, who became very upset. It wasn't just one slice; it was the whole pizza. That time I was really angry with him, and I banished him to the backyard for several minutes. I should say that the dogs loved the backyard, and I would never use banishment there as punishment. I just couldn't take Baylor's food thievery anymore. I needed a break.

We loved Baylor, so we didn't make a big deal out of his food thievery. That doesn't mean we accepted it, though. We did our best to keep people food out of his sight and reach, but we didn't always succeed. People food is not particularly conducive to a healthful dog diet, and unfortunately, Baylor developed diabetes. I had to give him insulin shots before every meal. But he was very cooperative, and he never complained despite the pinch he must have felt every time.

At this stage in Baylor's life Bronco had joined the family, and one day we witnessed what seemed like a miracle. Bronco started barking while looking at Baylor, then he intently looked at us, then he turned his head toward Baylor and started barking again. He did this a few times—not aggressively, but to get our attention. It became clear that Bronco wanted us to look at Baylor. I examined Baylor but saw nothing wrong at first. Then I looked again. This time I saw that his back legs were shaking slightly. It quickly got worse. His gait became wobbly, then within perhaps fifteen seconds he fainted. He had gone into insulin shock. We rushed him to the emergency clinic, where fortunately the doctors were able to revive him.[*]

Bronco detected a problem with Baylor before we could see anything wrong. His warnings gave us that little bit of extra time we needed to save Baylor's life. I still wonder what it was that Bronco noticed. Leonbergers have a very keen sense of smell, and people have told me that the dogs can smell when there's something physically wrong with a person. We had never taught Bronco to detect insulin shock or any other condition. It was entirely his own instinct. This was one of the amazing superpowers Bronco had.

Enter Baby

Baby was our second family dog. She was a German shepherd and was also a rescue. (Although we were told that she was a purebred, we didn't have a certificate.) First Claudia's sister Marianne adopted her, but when Marianne moved to France, we adopted Baby. Baylor and Baby became good friends, but sometimes Baby got annoyed with Baylor when he stole food, especially when it was hers. She liked to lie at the entrance to the kitchen and tell the other dogs, particularly Baylor, "You shall not pass." It wasn't because she wanted the

---

[*] We didn't know this at the time, but giving a dog sugar, or something sweet, can bring him out of insulin shock.

food for herself. She just didn't like other dogs stealing it, so she tried to prevent it, like a good kitchen police dog.

Baby was quiet and well behaved. She was well trained and easy to walk, but she wasn't fond of noisy places. She was a bit anxious and less social than our other dogs, and she didn't like dog parks, though she tolerated them. We were told that she had been mistreated by her first owners, and the first months of a dog's life are very important for his or her mental health.

Once when we were out visiting Claudia's parents for a Memorial Day dinner, before we got Bronco, our house was burglarized. We had left Baby and Baylor home alone in the backyard. The weather was nice, and we had put water bowls outside.

When we returned home and opened the front door, we were met by Baylor and Baby. We instantly knew something was wrong. How

Baby was always a little wary at the dog park.

did they get inside? We soon discovered evidence of the break-in. The burglars had entered through the garage. They had taken jewelry and a DVD player but left everything else. The losses were minor, and the thieves had apparently been very quick. We were a little disappointed that the dogs had not deterred the burglars. Baby was pretty protective, and she could look intimating when she wanted to. Why hadn't her presence stopped the burglars?

We called the police, and they wrote a report. They told us that the burglars were professionals who probably had been watching us for a while and knew how to handle our dogs. Usually, dogs are great for reducing the likelihood that your house will be broken into, because burglars want as little trouble as possible. Dogs can make it harder for unskilled burglars and random intruders—like the trespasser Bronco chased away.

However, according to the police, you should not entirely rely on dogs, even fierce dogs, to protect your property. Dogs are not entirely effective against professional burglars, who know how to appease them. I can imagine the burglars feeding the dogs medium-rare filet mignon or roast beef. They may even have befriended the dogs beforehand—who knows?

The police told us they couldn't do anything. The burglars left no trace of their efforts, and there were no witnesses. After that incident, we improved the security around our house—not just for us but also for the safety of our dogs.

A few of our dogs were really afraid of thunder and thunderstorms, and Baby was one of them. When we were out walking, and she heard thunder in the distance, she would start pulling the leash and telling me she wanted to go home. She had very good hearing, and she could tell when a thunderstorm was approaching long before I could. She also had a very good sense of direction, and she always knew the best route home, so I let her lead the way on those occasions.

Bronco, at the age of four or five months, would soon outgrow his playmate Baby.

Even though Baby was a shy and anxious dog at first, once we got Bronco, her personality changed. She loved Bronco, and she took on the job of being Bronco's adoptive mom. She played with him; she watched him; she was fiercely protective of him. Bronco was her puppy. She seemed rejuvenated, as if she had found an important job to do—a purpose, if you will. It was beautiful to see her take care of Bronco and play with him. She became happier and more confident, and Bronco loved her.

One day I was out walking with Baylor, Baby, and Bronco. Bronco was very young, maybe four months old. We met a man walking two medium-size black dogs off leash. Suddenly, one of the dogs attacked us. There was nothing I could do. As I watched helplessly, the black dog made the monumental mistake of going for Bronco. If the dog had attacked Baylor or Baby, either dog would certainly have put up a courageous defense, but going after Bronco was nearly suicidal—not because of Bronco himself but because of Baby.

I heard a loud explosion of barks that lasted only a few seconds, and then I saw the black dog flying five or six feet up into the air. Baby had bitten him in the side and tossed him skyward. It was surreal. I almost couldn't believe what I was witnessing.

The black dog lay in the street. The man knelt before him and started crying. He said his dog's back was broken. I was mortified, and I said, "I am so terribly sorry." He said, "It's not your fault. I was the one walking my dogs without a leash." It was gratifying for me to hear that under the circumstances, but it was no less tragic.

Then, to my astonishment, the black dog stood up and quickly walked back to the other side of the street. The dog was in shock, but he was fine. The man calmed down, and we said goodbye to each other on good terms.

It wasn't the only time Baby protected Bronco, but it was the most memorable. Thinking about it still sends chills down my spine. Years later, after Baylor and Baby passed and we got our small dogs, Bronco would take on the role of their protector. He would save lives.

On another occasion when I was walking Bronco and Baby, we met a man and his dog walking on the other side of the street, heading toward us. Bronco started barking at the dog, and the other dog responded. Both dogs worked themselves up into a frenzy. Bronco began pulling on his leash and even jumping. Baby remained quiet. But with all his carrying on, Bronco accidentally bumped Baby into a storm drain, which we happened to be standing right in front of.

To save Baby, I lay on my stomach and grabbed her around her

abdomen with one arm—all while holding Bronco's leash with my other hand. He continued pulling, jumping, and barking as I gradually dragged Baby up out of the drain. The guy on the other side of the street looked at us with big eyes, as if he had seen an evil clown peering out from the storm drain. He lifted his dog up in his arms and ran as fast as he could in the opposite direction.

Meanwhile, Bronco had calmed down, and I was able to drag Baby back onto the street. She loved Bronco, but after this incident she showed us in her own way that she'd rather not take her walks with him. We respected her wishes, and I walked them separately from that point on.

CHAPTER 5

Ryu and Daisy

Around a year after we got Bronco, we got a fourth dog, a Japanese Chin. He was a gift for our daughter, Rachel, who named him Ryu after a Japanese ninja warrior. Ryu was a very energetic dog, quick and brave—except that he was terrified of thunderstorms. At seventeen or eighteen pounds, he was bigger than most Japanese Chins, but he was still a small dog. He got along very well with Bronco.

We bought Ryu at Petland before we knew about the company's connection to puppy mills. So perhaps it wasn't a coincidence that soon after we bought him, when Claudia and Rachel walked into our local Petland with him to buy supplies, Ryu started shaking with fear. Claudia and Rachel decided to take him back outside. We don't know why he reacted that way. Maybe he thought he would be returned to the store. Maybe he associated the place with bad memories. The experience was certainly food for thought.

One of the things that stood out about Ryu was his singing. Japanese Chins are famous for their singing—well, actually, it's closer to howling, but Ryu's was a beautiful howl, and he was very proud of it.

As soon as he discovered that he got a lot of attention for it, he started doing it quite often. Whenever we came home, he would sit politely, look at us intently—it seemed like he was clearing his throat, too—and howl. Like an opera singer, he would slowly turn his head to look at us, as if he were performing. In fact I think Ryu's howling sounded just like a night at the opera—especially when the lyrics are sung in Italian.

We would say, "Good boy, Ryu," and clap, and he looked mighty proud. Other people thought it was cute and wonderful, too, and they gave him lots of praise, and of course he loved doing it and got good at it. When Rachel played the harmonica, Ryu would howl along. They made quite a duo.

"Good boy" might not be the kind of praise Andrea Bocelli would want, but Ryu was perfectly happy with it.

Ryu was also a good problem solver. For example, if he wanted a toy that was out of his reach, but he knew it was in the toy box, he would jump up on the side of the box to tip it over. After the box had spilled its contents, he would rummage through the toys on the floor until he found the one he wanted.

Because he was frequently around Bronco, who was protective of him, Ryu was sometimes overconfident, believing nothing bad could happen to him. One time, when he got outside, he attacked the neighbor's Doberman pinscher. To our great relief, the Doberman behaved, and Claudia was able to grab hold of Ryu fairly quickly.

The interaction between Ryu and Bronco was sometimes truly amazing to watch. I remember one instance in which Bronco was sleeping in the house and Ryu was outside in our fenced backyard. The door to the backyard was open. I heard Ryu bark a few times. He had evidently seen something he wanted us to notice—or something he wanted other people to notice.

Then I saw Ryu running in through the back door. He was a fast

Ryu, Bronco's loyal sidekick, was well known for his melodious voice.

runner. He ran to Bronco, jumped on his stomach, and barked at him. Bronco woke up, looking drowsy and confused. Ryu waited for Bronco to shake off his grogginess and get up, then he ran out the back door with Bronco in tow. They both hurried to the gate that leads to the street. Ryu yapped, and Bronco barked his loud, booming bark. Ryu had enlisted help to multiply his bark power.

Ryu was our most well-traveled dog. Claudia and I flew with him to visit Rachel at her out-of-state boarding school a couple of times. On both occasions we transported him in a special carry-on bag for dogs. Our airline allowed us to fly with a dog, provided that he weighed less than twenty pounds and that he'd had all his shots. After providing proof of his vaccination status from the veterinarian

Ryu and Rachel, who holds his paws in this photo, made a wonderful musical duo.

and paying a fee, we were able to stow the doggie carry-on bag under the seat in front of us. Ryu was very easy and quiet while he traveled. As a bonus, we discovered that the Atlanta airport is home to a small dog park.

On one trip to visit Rachel, Claudia stayed home, and I flew with Ryu. At the gate before boarding, a woman sitting next to me pointed to the bag and in a concerned voice said, "I saw the bag move." For a second, I thought about telling her, "Don't worry—I'm transporting snakes for the Dallas Zoo." (Have you seen the movie *Snakes on a Plane*? It's great.) However, I decided against that joke. I simply told her the truth: there was a small dog in the bag.

> ### Travel Tips
>
> If you're traveling by air with a small dog, you may want to buy a carrier that can fit under the seat in front of you—typically, this should be no more than 17.5 inches long, 12 inches wide, and 7.5 inches high. Bring your dog's immunization records with you.
>
> If you're traveling with a Leonberger, obviously he won't be eligible for a seat in the cabin. But you can check your Leonberger as baggage or use a cargo service. If you're making a trip overland, you can take a train. If you're flying overseas, you may need to get your dog a pet passport from your veterinarian. There may also be customs rules you need to be aware of in the country you're traveling to. Remember to take climate, accommodations, and legal issues into account as well. For example, you don't want to take a big furry Leonberger to a place that's extremely hot. A good source of information regarding traveling with dogs is PetTravel.com.

Wake Up, Little Daisy, You're Late for the Couch

All our children were allowed to choose a dog when they were growing up—but only when they were old enough to understand that it's a big responsibility. Jacob picked Bronco, Rachel picked Ryu, and David, our middle child, picked Daisy, a pug. However, our dogs were never just birthday presents. We made sure everyone understood that getting a dog is a years-long commitment that cannot be reversed. We needed to make sure we could give each dog a good life before we would consider making this commitment.

Daisy arrived the year after we got Ryu. Like Ryu, she was pur-

For Daisy, it's tongue-out Tuesday every day.

chased at Petland. Daisy is now thirteen years old and in good health at the time of this writing. She's an easygoing, funny dog with an unusually long tongue, and everyone loves her, dogs as well as people. When it comes to being liked, she doesn't have to try—she's a natural. Ryu and Daisy would become best friends, but they also got along well with our other dogs. Daisy loved to follow Ryu around, and together they often trailed Bronco wherever he went. Pugs are not very energetic or fast, but they have easygoing and cheerful personalities. When the other dogs were being annoying, she liked to hide under chairs and tables to avoid getting involved.

Daisy is a bit of couch potato—a very sweet couch potato. She sits

Daisy rests after an exhausting day on the bed and sofa, not quite finished doing nothing.

on the sofa most of the day, watching TV or looking out the window. She barks at dogs on TV or passersby outside, but other than that she doesn't move much. She likes to snuggle, sit in your lap, and sleep with her head resting on your leg or arm. What with our beds, the dog beds, the sofas, and our backyard, she sure has a lot of places to relax. The only thing missing is her glass of wine.*

Ryu used to get jealous when other dogs gave Daisy attention, or so it seemed. For example, he would become hostile to any dog in the dog park who began playing with Daisy. What can I say? She's Miss Congeniality.

Daisy is the only dog I've met who really enjoys sunbathing. Our

---

* I'm joking. Don't ever give dogs alcohol.

When it's hot outside, Daisy loves to sunbathe. When it's cold, she sits in front of the heating vents.

backyard isn't exactly Playa Grande, but she frequently goes outside and lies down on her back. While our other dogs easily get too hot outside, she just soaks up the sun.

Other than following Ryu out on an adventure a couple of times and running out to say hello to Lily, a pug mix who used to live across the street, Daisy will not wander off. On the few occasions she did, we just called her back. She likes being home; she likes the couch and the safety of our house. And while our other dogs sometimes ignored our commands, Daisy never does. Another thing that's different about her is that she doesn't like cheese.

Ryu, too, loved the security of the house. In fact every time we made preparations to travel, he and Daisy seemed to sense it. As soon as we so much as took out our suitcases, they knew what was going on. You could see it in their faces and in the way they behaved. They were a bit sad.

One time, as we were packing our bags, we turned around and saw

Ryu and Daisy didn't want us to leave for our trip.

the scene I captured in the photo on page 51. How would you interpret this? Was it a protest? Did they want to come with us? Maybe both.

In what may have been a sign of anxiety during our absence, we once came home from a brief family outing and Daisy greeted us at the front door with a tissue box over her head. While we had been gone, she had somehow gotten her head stuck in it and couldn't get it off. She was still running around barking. We laughed because it was such a funny sight, but she probably didn't enjoy the experience. We removed it quickly.

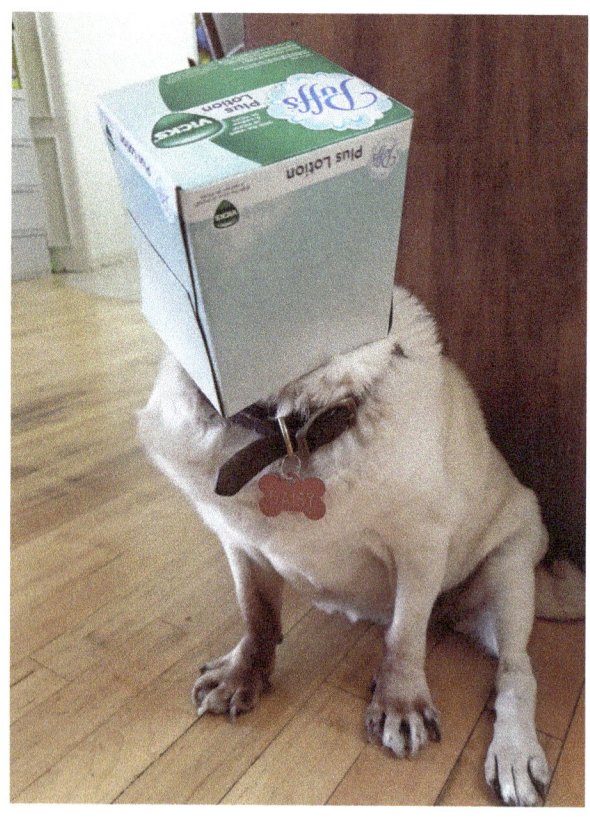

We still don't know how Daisy managed this feat.

Ryu and Daisy

As Daisy has gotten older, she's slowed down. She's never been fast, and she's always had a hard time walking long distances, especially in the heat. She loves her walks, and she loves sniffing, but to give her a break now and then, we bought her a stroller. As long as she gets to walk some of the way and do some sniffing, she doesn't seem to mind. She seems to think that sitting in the stroller, rolling through

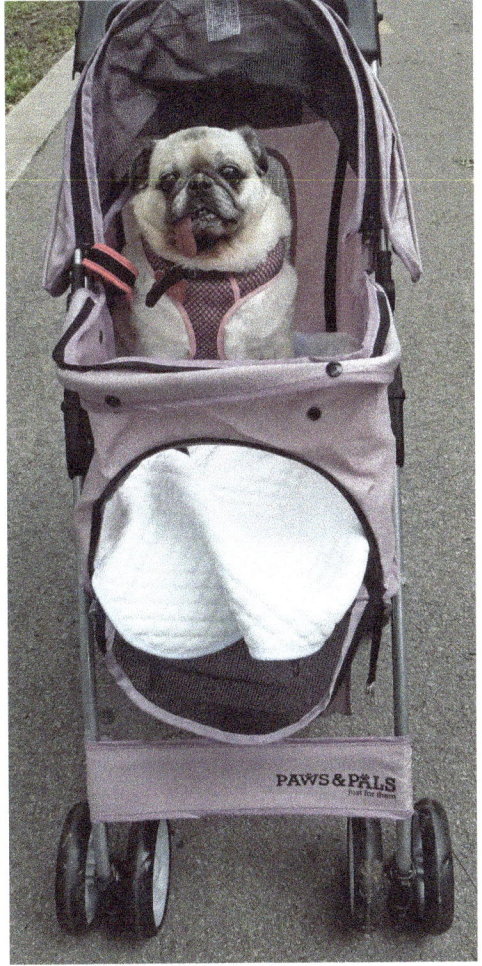

Daisy poses in her royal chariot.

the neighborhood and watching what's going on, is an adventure in itself.

The Importance of Identification

One afternoon, Claudia got a phone call from a woman who had found a small black-and-white dog walking around the streets of North Dallas with a pug following close behind. She thought they looked hilarious, but she realized that this was hardly a good situation and decided to help. She rounded up the dogs, checked their tags, and called us, for which we were very grateful. It wasn't the first time Ryu and Daisy had escaped, and it worried us. We couldn't figure out how they managed to do it.

Then one day I caught them in the act. At the back of the area in our yard that we call the dog run, there is a concrete wall, and by the corner of that wall there used to be a hole in the fence, a bit above the wall. I had never noticed it before because it was hidden and pretty small. Ryu and Daisy would jump up on the wall at its lowest spot, then walk down the wall to the fence, then climb up a bit on the fence and slink through the hole. Of course, after seeing that, I fixed the hole.

For us, this incident underscored the importance of identification, which greatly increases the chances that your dog will be returned to you if he's lost. At a minimum, you should put a traditional dog tag, available at most pet stores, on his collar, containing his name and your contact information. You should also consider microchipping and/or tattooing.

When your dog is microchipped,[*] a veterinarian uses a syringe to

---

[*] Jan Reisen, "How Do Microchips Work and Should My Dog Have One?," American Kennel Club, April 14, 2021, at https://www.akc.org/expert-advice/lifestyle/how-do-dog-microchips-work/.

insert a small scannable computer chip, which uses radio frequency identification (RFID) technology, under his skin.* It has no internal power source: instead, the handheld scanner that reads the chip energizes its capacitor, which then sends signals back to the scanner. The scanner and the chip both use a specific frequency, and those frequencies must match in order for the reading to work. It is recommended that you use a microchip that can be read by a universal scanner.

When your dog is tattooed, a veterinarian inks the relevant information onto an area that is readily visible, such as the ear, so whoever finds your dog can easily identify him. Since a thief very easily can remove a tag, it's a good idea to have either a microchip or a tattoo in addition to a tag. We opted for tags and microchips for all our dogs.

There is no national law requiring dogs to be licensed and/or registered, but most county and municipal governments have those requirements. That includes our city of Dallas, which requires all dogs to be microchipped and to have regular rabies vaccinations. There is also an associated registration fee of around thirty dollars. If you don't do this for your pet, at least in our area, you're breaking the law.

---

* "Separating Microchipping Facts from Fiction," HomeAgain, at https://www.homeagain.com/microchipping-facts.html.

CHAPTER 6

Adventures in the Backyard and Beyond

Bronco loved playing and jumping around in our backyard, which we were happy to let him do. A fenced-in backyard is generally a secure place for a dog, but beware—there may be hazards present that you aren't aware of.

One day Bronco came running into the house with a large piece of skin hanging from his stomach. It was around two feet long and maybe a foot wide, and the exposed flesh was bleeding. It looked horrible, and I almost thought I was going to faint when I saw it. But Claudia kept a cool head, and she quickly wrapped a towel around him to hold the skin on. Then we rushed him to the veterinary clinic.

Bronco was very cooperative. The wound must have hurt, but he understood that he was being helped and calmly accepted all treatment. Fortunately, the cuts were not deep. All he needed was stitches—a lot of them—but in the end he was fine.

We soon discovered what had happened. In our backyard there is a decorative brick wall. It was there when we bought the house. But the corner piece had begun to disintegrate from age and the effects of the weather. The bricks were crumbling, baring a metal rod that was hidden inside.

After this incident, we had someone cut off the rod as soon as possible. I had not realized that sometimes there are metal rods inside even short brick walls for support. If the rod somehow becomes exposed, you have a hazard that's dangerous to dogs and children. I learned that there are many potential dangers *inside* houses, too, but backyards and garages are often filled with hidden perils.

Hazards at Home

The backyard can be a great place for dogs to spend time, but it can also be a dangerous place for them, and you should inspect it regularly. Dogs, especially puppies, may chew on toxic plants, including aloe, lily, elephant ear, and others.[*] Determine what kind of plantings you have and research them to determine whether they're poisonous.

If you have a pool, check to see whether a dog can get out of it by himself. Walk around the house and yard and make sure the environment is safe. Are there any objects sticking up out of the grass? Can wild animals such as bobcats and coyotes get in through your fence? And if you can't safeguard the garage, don't allow the dog in there.

Inside the house, too, there are several potential dangers. Below is a partial list of indoor hazards to consider.

LIVING ROOM
- Toxic houseplants
- Fireplace
- Glass tables, large vases, things that can easily tip and fall

[*] Cornell College of Agriculture and Life Sciences, "Poisonous Plants Affecting Dogs," at https://poisonousplants.ansci.cornell.edu/dogs/index.html, and "Ten Tips for a Poison-Safe Household," at https://poisonousplants.ansci.cornell.edu/dogs/ten_tips.html.

KITCHEN
- Chocolate
- Coffee beans
- Onions
- Garbage
- Food left out

BATHROOM
- Toilet-bowl additives
- Drain cleaners
- Medication
- Bar soap
- Tampons

GARAGE
- Paint
- Antifreeze
- Pesticides
- Oil and gasoline
- Rat poison
- Carpet cleaner
- Fertilizer

LAUNDRY ROOM
- Bleach
- Detergent
- Hot iron

ALL ROOMS
- Sharp objects
- Glass jars
- Electrical cords

Bronco the Escape Artist

When Bronco was young, he could be a bit of an escape artist. In fact, one day when he was around a year old, I heard scratching at the front door. I opened it, and there stood Bronco, who calmly walked right in as if it were the most normal thing in the world. We had no idea he had been outside.

How did he get out? All the doors were closed and locked. I checked the fence around the yard—the gate was closed, and there were no holes in it. No one called to complain about a big dog roaming the neighborhood.

When I was a college student, I took a class in quantum physics and learned that there is such a thing as quantum tunneling, in which a particle ends up on the other side of a wall without traveling through it. It seemed like Bronco was capable of quantum tunneling, too. However he got out, it remains a mystery.

Three of our escape artists stand ready for their next adventure.

On one side of our house, we have a secluded fenced-in area that we call the dog run—a strip of concrete that runs alongside the house, punctuated on one side with a patch of grass where a tree and a small bush grow. So the dogs could go out when we weren't home, we installed a fairly large dog door that led from our laundry room to this outdoor strip (but not to the backyard itself). The door was made for Baylor and Baby, but it was a little too small for Bronco.

Amazingly, though, Bronco was able to get through it. One day I saw how he did it, and it was a sight to behold. He lay down flat on his belly and dragged himself in and out through the door while grasping for the edges with his paws, as a human would do—and as I had done one day when I locked myself out of the house.

Claudia felt that the size of the dog door was a potential security issue. She pointed out that if Bronco and I could crawl in and out through it, a burglar could, too. So we replaced it with a smaller one, which meant that Bronco, Baylor, and Baby no longer had access to the outdoors when we weren't home. But we all adjusted to the new situation—and I made sure I didn't lock myself out of the house again.

A couple of times, Bronco took advantage of the fact that the snap hook on his leash would come loose and detach from his collar. One day this became a big problem. Bronco ran off, and I chased him—across the street, across people's lawns, across the street again, and back over neighboring lawns. When he ran in circles, I ran in circles right behind him, yelling at him. He would stop and wait for me, and then as soon as I got close, he would start running again. I even jumped to catch him a few times. But he dashed off both times, and I just landed flat on my belly.

Bronco had a lot of fun doing this. I imagined him laughing at me, and I got angry. Dogs can't laugh, of course, but his tail was wagging in excitement, and it was obviously a game to him—a dangerous game.

So I asked him, "Do you want to be lost? Bad things happen to dogs who get lost." I don't know how much of that he understood, but I had to tell him the truth. Then I turned around and started walking home. I figured I'd never catch him, so it was better for me to go back and get help. (It was 2008, and I didn't have a cell phone.) Naturally, I worried that Bronco would get hit by a car. I was also worried about the damage an energetic 130-pound adolescent dog could do to the neighborhood.

As I stomped off, I turned around to look at Bronco. He stood still, around a hundred yards away, staring back at me. He seemed confused. I continued walking. After a while, I heard the soft slapping of big paws on the road behind me, accompanied by some distinctly noisy breathing. Then I saw Bronco walking next to me, so I carefully snapped the leash back onto his collar. He let me do it without protest. He was finished playing games. We walked home calmly, and the next day I bought a new and better leash.

But Bronco never lost his sense of adventure. He learned quickly how to lift a latch and push a gate open. One day when we were at the dog park, he opened the gates when I wasn't paying attention. I heard someone shout, "Look—that dog is letting all the dogs out!" So I ran over to the gates and got hold of him, brought him back in, and closed the gate so the other dogs couldn't escape.

As it turns out, though, Bronco wasn't really trying to escape from the dog park. He was trying to get into the area where the small dogs play—the ones who weigh less than twenty-five pounds. That's where Ryu and Daisy were playing with Claudia and Rachel. He just wanted to be with his family.

At the dog park, a young Bronco figured out how to lift the latch to the gate around the play area.

The Fauna of North Dallas

It happened quite often that Bronco and our other dogs discovered animals—cats, rabbits, and opossums, mostly—hidden underneath bushes or in tall grass in our neighborhood. I would never have seen these animals if my dogs hadn't attempted to chase them.

I'll never forget the time Bronco almost ripped my arm out of its socket when he went after a cat hiding in a bush. It was only after I face-planted in the bush that I saw the cat, which Bronco had smelled two seconds earlier. The same thing happened while I was walking Baylor. One of our neighbors often left cat food hidden in the bushes for their cats, who spent a considerable amount of time outdoors. I had no idea there was food there—but the dogs knew. I apologize to any and all cat owners whose food was stolen, but my dogs were quicker than I was.

I remember once when a couple in a car was slowly passing by me and Bronco during one of our walks. A rabbit ran across our path, and Bronco gave chase. I was not ready, and I almost fell forward. As I was trying to gain a foothold, Bronco dragged me across the neighbors' lawns. The rabbit was leading the train: Bronco came after the rabbit, and I was at the end of the leash stumbling and shouting at Bronco to stop. The couple in the car stopped—not because they wanted to help me but because they were laughing uncontrollably.

Our neighborhood is generously populated with coyotes as well as rabbits. Bronco used to bark at them, so they never got close to us. I assume they were afraid of him, but they certainly weren't afraid of Daisy or Ryu.

One day I saw a coyote coming around the corner at the end of our street as I was walking Daisy and Ryu. He saw us and proceeded straight toward us without hesitation and with no sign of fear. He wasn't running, but coyotes have long legs, and he was sort of trotting along and moving pretty fast. I wasn't worried for myself—an adult human can easily handle a lone coyote. I was worried for Daisy and Ryu. I didn't want them to be the coyote's dinner.

As the coyote came closer, I stopped and stared at him. When he was around fifteen feet away, he stopped and stared back at me. Ryu and Daisy were staring at the coyote, too. I could see that they were frightened, but they didn't bark.

Meanwhile, I was calculating how best I could fight the animal. It wasn't practical to lift both dogs in my arms and try to fight at the same time. So I had to let the dogs stay on the ground.

Before I could strategize further, though, the coyote continued on his way and disappeared behind some houses farther down the road.

Coyotes are pretty common almost everywhere in the United States, so if you need another reason avoid letting your cats and small dogs run loose, remind yourself of this story.

CHAPTER 7

Adventures in the Backyard and Beyond Part II

One thing all our dogs loved was going for a car ride. The big dogs loved sticking their heads out the window and feeling the wind in their faces. The little dogs loved going places. And they all loved looking at the passing scenery. Oh, the things you can see when you're "ridin' in the car, car," as the Woody Guthrie song goes!

There were some sights that got the dogs especially excited. They would bark if they saw people working on roofs or riding bicycles, for example. They would become even more animated if we got close to a dog park or a McDonald's drive-through window. (That might have been because sometimes we bought them snacks at the McDonald's drive-through.)

One time when I was taking Bronco, Baylor, and Baby to the dog park, a car passing me slowed down and started driving right next to me. I looked over, slightly annoyed, and saw that the people in the car were pointing at us and laughing. I was thinking, "What is their problem?" Then I glanced back at the dogs and realized that we did look funny. Bronco was sitting in the front passenger seat with his head close to the roof, looking majestic. Baylor and Baby were sitting in their own seats in the back. They probably looked like human passengers from a distance, but as the people in the car got closer, they realized that the heads weren't human heads but dogs' heads and burst out laughing.

Bronco the Great Swimmer

Leonbergers are double-coated, and they have webbed paws, so they're natural swimmers. Bronco was no exception: he loved to swim and chase waterfowl at our go-to destination, White Rock Lake. If he saw ducks or egrets in the water, he would swim after them. They would fly off before he could get to them, though, so he

---

Car Safety for Dogs

There are several options for traveling securely with your dog in the car.[*] Perhaps the safest choice is to use a travel crate. If you have a van or large SUV, you can put the crate in the cargo space, or you can use a pet gate to keep the dog from jumping into the passenger area. You might also want to get a ramp so the dog can walk into the back of the vehicle and you don't have to lift him. Bronco was not comfortable with the ramp: I think it felt flimsy to him, so we just let him jump in the car instead.

Another option is to use seat-belt harnesses. They're easy to find. One end is a latch plate that fits into the seat belt buckle in the car. The other end is a snap hook that you hook to the back of the harness.

* Michael Stonewood, *The Leonberger: A Complete and Comprehensive Owners Guide to Buying, Owning, Health, Grooming, Training, Obedience, Understanding, and Caring for Your Leonberger* (self-pub., 2019), 61.

never caught any. That was okay—he still had fun, and he had no egrets (pun intended).

Claudia started taking Bronco to White Rock with Baylor and Baby when he was an adolescent. At first, he was hesitant to get into the water. Then a nice man came along (we don't know who he was) and threw a stick a little way out into the lake. He asked Bronco to get it, and he did. Then he threw the stick a little bit farther so that Bronco had to swim to get it. Little by little and step by step, the man encouraged Bronco to swim. And once he got started, there was no looking back. Swimming in the lake became one of his favorite pastimes.

After a while, getting Bronco into the water was easy. Unleash him,

---

When you go for car rides, don't forget to bring water and water bowls—and, of course, your leashes.

As everyone knows, dogs love to put their heads out car windows. Perhaps the wind feels good to them. Bronco, Baylor, and Baby—but especially Bronco—loved doing this. Bronco wanted the window open all the time. I was always a bit uncomfortable with this. Sometimes pebbles shoot up from the road or fly off truck tires and can hit the dogs. If you use a harness, that won't happen, of course.

We hardly ever left the dogs in the car. We did a few times, when the weather was cool and the car was parked in a safe and monitored location. But leaving dogs in cars is extremely dangerous for two reasons. First, if it's warm outside, they can get heatstroke, which can be fatal. There is also a risk that they can be stolen. So as a general rule, leave the dogs at home when you go shopping.

and he would walk right in. Getting Bronco out—that was another story.

It wasn't that he disobeyed. He came out of the water when we asked him to. The problem was what happened after he came out. He shook himself dry, like all wet dogs do, but a large dog with a coat like his has a lot of water to share. If you've ever been to a show at SeaWorld, you know that you get very wet if you sit in the first row. It was the same with Bronco: if you stood close enough to hold the leash, you were bound to get soaked when he shook himself. Our choices were to walk away, hide behind a tree, or take the involuntary bucket challenge. Towels certainly came in handy.

One morning, Claudia was taking Bronco for a walk around the lake with two of her sisters, Dora and Marianne. Suddenly Bronco jumped in the lake. But there were steep banks on either side of him, and he couldn't get back out. So Claudia got in the water with him

Leonbergers are excellent swimmers and are sometimes used in water rescue.

Adventures in the Backyard and Beyond Part II 69

Bronco loved swimming in White Rock Lake.

and pushed his butt while Dora and Marianne encouraged him to move toward a less steep part of the bank. They got him out, but this scary incident didn't decrease Bronco's love of swimming.

Bronco Gets the Attention

Bronco was used to getting a lot of attention, and he loved it. He wanted to say hello to every dog and every human who crossed his path. Whenever people came into the dog park, for example, he ran to greet them and sniff them. This was not always appreciated by everyone because he was so big, but typically it was not a problem. Most people and other dogs could see that he was friendly.

There was one instance, however, in which this greeting didn't go well. On that day I saw two teenage girls approaching the dog park, which seemed odd because they didn't have any dogs with them. One of them looked very nervous—probably because she was afraid of dogs—and the other was pushing her along. My guess is that this was some kind of dare or perhaps a misguided way of overcoming fear.

As these thoughts ran through my mind, I wondered, Where is Bronco? But it was too late. I saw him running toward the gate, and as soon as the girls unlatched it and walked in, he greeted them enthusiastically. He jumped up and put his big paws on the shoulders of the fearful girl and licked her face. She gave a little shriek. I grabbed Bronco and apologized, and the other girl comforted her. She calmed down, and then they walked through the dog park as if it were a minefield and back out on the other side.

One of the advantages of having a Leonberger is that they attract attention. Leonbergers are big, impressive, and good looking, and they seem affectionate. During our walks, Bronco often pulled me toward people he wanted to meet. He sniffed them and said hello in his doggie way, and he loved it when they talked to him and petted him in return. I frequently had to apologize and say, "Sorry—sometimes he's overly friendly." Usually, people responded well and said nice things like "He's so beautiful."

But people generally aren't familiar with Leonbergers and can't identify them when they see them. So the two questions I got most often were "What breed is he?" and "Is that a mutt?" To people who asked the former question, I responded, "He's a Leonberger," and let them pet Bronco. But to people who asked the latter question, I responded, "No," and didn't let them pet Bronco. Just because you don't recognize the breed doesn't mean the dog is a mutt. There are rare and noble breeds not everyone recognizes. There are also people who do recognize the breed, and that's impressive. I love mutts, too, just as much as purebreds, but it feels good when a rare purebred dog is recognized for what he is.

Once, when Jacob was walking Bronco, a car pulled up next to them and a woman and her teenage daughter got out. They asked if they could take pictures with Bronco. Jacob said yes, and the girl excitedly stood next to Bronco while the mom took photos. They didn't want Jacob in the picture—just Bronco—but they were very nice and asked about his breed.

Bronco liked to get attention at home, too, especially if he was hungry. He would come over to you, lift his paw, and poke you in your chest with it. When he got older and didn't get up as often, he liked to slam his paw on the floor to get attention.

"Hey, Dad—it's dinnertime."

Bronco wasn't too interested in playing with balls. Leonbergers are bored by repetition, so throwing a ball and asking Bronco to bring it back to us only worked a couple of times. He was more of an independent thinker, and he loved toys that made sounds. He loved squeezing his toy ducks and shaking them. If you threw one toward him, he would catch it in midair. He was quite good at catching things you threw for him.

Sometimes Bronco's playfulness attracted attention that was not completely positive. For example, don't give a big dog a big bone at 11:00 p.m., especially if you have wooden floors. Bronco loved to chew these bones, noisily, then lift them up and drop them on the floor. What a marvelously loud noise that made! He would do that over . . . and over . . . and over . . . "Let's have a loud midnight bone party that shakes the whole house!" When that happened, you could just give up on sleeping.

INTERMEZZO

Baylor and Baby Pass

Whenever we went on vacation or on an extended trip, the dogs didn't like it. It's not hard to understand why: dogs don't like being left behind. So we always tried our best to find good solutions. We found that having a pet sitter stay at our house was the best and safest alternative, yet from the dogs' perspective, nothing is as good as your staying at home with them.

In December of 2008, we were planning a one-week trip. Baylor was maybe twelve years old at this point, and Bronco was a year and a half. We also had Baby and Ryu (but not yet Daisy) at home. We needed someone to watch our dogs while we were gone. Following a recommendation from our veterinarian at the time, we settled for a sitter who would visit the dogs, feed them, and walk them but not stay at our house full-time. This sounded like the best option at the time, but it turned out to be a disaster.

After we left on our trip, we got a phone call from the sitter, who told us that she was taking care of several other dogs in addition to ours and that she did not have time to drive back and forth to our house and attend to our dogs. The fact she was taking care of several other dogs simultaneously was news to us. She asked if she could take our four dogs to her house. She stated that she had a fence like ours, and by having them at her house she could watch them 100 percent of the time.

We didn't really like the idea because the dogs had never stayed at someone else's house before. Moreover, we had never seen her house and we had no idea how crowded it was with the other dogs there. But it sounded like the best solution under the circumstances, so we reluctantly agreed.

A couple of days later, the dog sitter called us again, but this time she told us that Baylor was missing. He had been barking at night, so she put him out in the backyard. Unfortunately, the gate at her place had been left open, and she didn't notice that Baylor was gone until early in the morning. She asked us what we thought she should do.

We told her that she had to find him. "Go look for him; put up posters," we said. She was reluctant to do any of that because she didn't want to leave the other dogs alone. We told her that it was an emergency and she had to do it. We suggested that she recruit other people to help her. Baylor had to be found.

We were pretty upset about the fact that the sitter had put Baylor out into the backyard in the middle of a cold night and left him there. However, we needed her help, so we kept calm. We enlisted help from family members in Dallas, and I used an online service called My Lost Pet Alert, which sent 2,264 emails to people in our neighborhood that night. It didn't help that it was cold and sleeting and the

Intermezzo: Baylor and Baby Pass

streets were icy and dark. Baylor also needed his insulin shot in the morning.

The following afternoon Baylor was found dead two miles from the dog sitter's place. He had been hit by a car. He was found around midway between her house and our house, so it seemed like he was trying to get home.

Baylor had a very special place in our hearts, and I was devastated. Claudia was crying, and the kids were crying. Not only had we lost a family member in a sudden cruel twist of fate, but his death was also likely an unpleasant one. That it was the result of a dog sitter's carelessness didn't make it any better. In fact, it made it worse.

Should we have sued the sitter? Our vacation was certainly ruined, and for a long time, it felt like our lives were, too. Our younger kids still cried over this incident years later. However, what would a lawsuit do? We certainly wished that we had never left our dogs with this person. The driver who hit Baylor and just left him there was another disappointment.

I think the story of Baylor's passing carries a lesson for all dog owners. If you're going on a trip and must leave your dogs, make sure you leave them with people who you know can care for them safely. I can think of a few options:

- leave them at a reputable dog hotel or kennel;
- let someone you trust dog sit at your house day and night;
- leave them with a close relative you trust;

- leave them with a dog sitter who isn't taking care of other dogs at the same time and who has an escape-proof fence guaranteed to be closed and locked at all times;
- check for yourself: don't trust recommendations.

Dogs will want to escape from a strange place. So we should have said no the first time the sitter called us. We should have told her that

---

The Rainbow Bridge

According to an article in the *Washington Post*,* the Rainbow Bridge is "a mythical overpass said to connect heaven and earth—and, more to the point, a spot where grieving pet owners reunite for good with their departed furry friends." It's also a poem of unknown origin that spawned a pet-bereavement movement and even a worldwide Pet Remembrance Day, August 28. The poem in its entirety follows.

Just this side of heaven is a place called Rainbow Bridge. When an animal dies that has been especially close to someone here, that pet goes to Rainbow Bridge. There are meadows and hills for all of our special friends so they can run and play together. There is plenty of food, water, and sunshine, and our friends are warm and comfortable.

* Ann Marie Gardner, "What Is the Rainbow Bridge and Why Do We Think Dead Pets Cross It?," *Washington Post*, May 1, 2018, at https://www.washingtonpost.com/news/animalia/wp/2018/05/01/what-is-the-rainbow-bridge-and-why-do-we-think-dead-pets-cross-it/; also see "Rainbow Bridge Poem," at https://www.rainbowsbridge.com/Poem.htm.

taking the dogs to her house wasn't what we agreed upon and that she needed to come up with another solution.

I believe that life will eventually leave each one of us with some regrets. This is one of ours—something we will always wish that we'd never done.

> *All the animals who had been ill and old are restored to health and vigor. Those who were hurt or maimed are made whole and strong again, just as we remember them in our dreams of days and times gone by. The animals are happy and content, except for one small thing: they each miss someone very special to them who had to be left behind.*
>
> *They all run and play together, but the day comes when one suddenly stops and looks into the distance. His bright eyes are intent. His eager body quivers. Suddenly he begins to run from the group, flying over the green grass, his legs carrying him faster and faster.*
>
> *You have been spotted, and when you and your special friend finally meet, you cling together in joyous reunion, never to be parted again. The happy kisses rain upon your face; your hands again caress the beloved head, and you look once more into the trusting eyes of your pet, so long gone from your life but never absent from your heart.*
>
> *Then you cross Rainbow Bridge together.*

Around one year later, we lost our German shepherd, Baby. She was very old at the time, perhaps as old as seventeen. It was discovered during a routine veterinary exam that she had a tumor in her belly, but it was thought to be benign. One of the veterinarians we were using for Baby suggested surgery, and we agreed.

This turned out to be a mistake. Baby had malignant tumors as well, so the surgery turned out to be pointless. Also, the anesthesia caused her to have a stroke soon thereafter. She quickly got sicker, and she started to lose her ability to walk.

We realized that we were going to have to euthanize her, but we hesitated. Why not give her as much life as possible? Claudia was

Intermezzo: Baylor and Baby Pass

You have left our lives but you will never leave our heart

scheduled to go on a weekend trip to visit a friend, and we decided to wait to make the decision until she came back.

Because Baby had a hard time walking, we created a makeshift sling by sliding a towel under her belly and holding it up by the ends in order to keep her upright and reduce the stress on her legs. I hired a dog walker to help me: the plan was that we would take turns holding her with the towel. He came over on a Friday afternoon, and I showed him how it worked so he could start helping me the next morning.

Friday night, Baby went to sleep on her mattress. But by the next morning, she was dead. The dog walker showed up on time,

at 8:00 a.m. on Saturday, but I had to tell him that Baby had died during the night. I offered to pay him, but he declined.

On the one hand, it felt like a relief to not have to put Baby down. On the other hand, I felt bad that she died the way she did. Euthanasia is an entirely painless and peaceful way of dying, and Baby probably did not need the suffering she experienced in the last few days of her life. I sometimes wonder about her last night on earth. Did she sleep? Was she in pain? I didn't hear her make any sounds.

Instead of hesitating, Claudia and I should have realized that Baby was not going to get better and that the best thing to do was end her suffering sooner rather than later. That's another one of our regrets.

CHAPTER 8

Gustatory and Other Perils

Have you ever wondered how dog food tastes to dogs? Is the flavor of kibble satisfying? Or is it boring and tasteless? If you let dogs choose between a medium-rare fillet and the dry but highly recommended Science Diet, you'll see.

I once conducted an experiment. I put antelope backstrap and sausage in one bowl and regular dry dog food in another. It may come as a shock, but our dogs preferred the antelope. In fact, after eating it, they wouldn't touch the dry food. I also tasted the dry food myself, then I wrote a review. So many people write reviews of dog food without tasting it first. Okay—I admit that my tasting of the dry food was a peculiar joke, and I did it only once, but I think my dog food review stood out.

Sometimes, especially when our dogs didn't feel well, it was impossible to get them to eat their regular dry food. So our veterinarian recommended that we sprinkle Parmesan cheese on top. I found out later that this is often recommended by veterinarians to make food more palatable. It worked well with all our dogs except Daisy, who doesn't like cheese.

A handyman working in our house once saw me doing this. He looked at me with a concerned expression and said, "Thomas, you're fired." He just couldn't believe I was putting Parmesan cheese on dog food. I tried to convince him that it was okay, and I might have succeeded.

But the culinary exploits of Bronco and the other dogs went much further than just Parmesan cheese. Bronco, especially, was so big that he could easily steal food from tall counters and high pantry shelves. However, he was not as hungry or as bold as Baylor, so he stole food less often. But when he did, it could be spectacular.

One day while we were gone, Bronco raided the kitchen and the pantry in what must have been a record haul. Imagine eating a box of pastries, a loaf of bread, a grilled chicken, a container of mashed potatoes, a Key lime pie, and a plate of scraps after eating a two-pound bag of dog treats. He was on a diet at the time.

Then, one evening when I came home from work, I saw a group of people standing in the street, laughing and shouting. In the middle of the crowd was Bronco, and right behind him were Daisy and Ryu. Our neighbor was having a party, and the guests had come out to feed hors d'oeuvres to the dogs. I don't know how the dogs got out, but we suspect that one of the party guests had opened the gate, which was closed but unlocked that day.[*]

One woman stretched out her hand to Bronco, offering him an hors d'oeuvre, and he happily snatched it out of her fingers. She jumped and squealed and ran off laughing, looking very proud of herself. Bronco, Ryu, and Daisy were certainly party animals that evening. But this was not a good situation, and I had to step in and ruin their good time by bringing them back home.

---

[*] Later, we found out that Bronco could open an unlocked gate by shaking it hard for a long time until the latch flew open.

Gustatory and Other Perils

You can see traces of Bronco's gluttony on the fur around his muzzle.

A few doors down from our veterinary clinic was a pet store full of dog snacks of all kinds. One day we took Bronco there after a visit to the clinic, and so began a new tradition: after every visit he dragged us to the pet store, and we bought him a little snack. He trained us well. It was not a bad thing because it made it easy to take him to the veterinarian without any protests.

The open gate behind Daisy and Bronco permitted their gingerbread-house raid.

On another occasion, Rachel made a gingerbread house and left it on the kitchen counter. I had forgotten to lock the kitchen gate, and the photograph above shows what greeted me when I got home. Guess who ate half the gingerbread house. I should say that Bronco shared some with Daisy. He was always very generous.

On yet another occasion, Bronco got hold of a box of chocolates in the shape of small gnomes. Each gnome was filled with liquor—some with gin, some with vodka, some with whiskey, and some with rum. It was a gift from Rachel, who had just come back from a visit to China. She had bought the present for us at the airport in Hong

Kong. But Bronco ate the entire thing—tinfoil wrappers, chocolate, liquor, and all. We were afraid he might get very sick, and we carefully monitored him, ready to rush him to the emergency clinic if necessary. Fortunately, nothing happened, except he threw up a little bit of tinfoil. I guess he had a stomach of steel.

I have to say our dogs ate well. We sometimes took them to dog-friendly restaurants such as Neuhaus Café, which allowed dogs on the patio. Our dogs loved going there. We usually bought them turkey sausage, turkey bacon, chicken, hot dogs, or another snack. Neuhaus provided cold water for them, and the waiters were very nice to them. Customers and passersby would come over and pet the dogs, too, which the dogs loved, especially Bronco. And on their birthdays, they always got some special treats—but only if they wore a hat.

Daisy prepares to enjoy her hamburger at Neuhaus Café.

Birthday celebrations always call for a special hat.

It's Daisy's birthday, but Bronco wants some of her "cake."

What to Feed Your Leonberger—
and What Not to Feed Him

Dry food, or kibble, is one option often recommended for Leonbergers. A puppy as young as eight weeks can eat dry food if it's moistened with a little bit of water or canned food. But a puppy shouldn't be given dry food with too much protein in it, because this can accelerate his growth, resulting in a condition called panosteitis.[*] You can buy dry food tailored for various ages, sizes, and breeds. Look for packages that have an AAFCO (Association of American Food Control Officials) statement on them, because this ensures that the food has the proper nutritional value. It's best if the food contains real meat, such as beef, chicken, or lamb.

There are alternatives to dry food, such as the meat-and-biscuit[†] diet and tripe.[‡] We never tried these alternatives, and our veterinarian never recommended them, but many people claim that tripe is better for dogs than mass-manufactured dry food and that the meat-and-biscuit diet is a healthful and tasty alternative.

Leonbergers should be fed at least twice a day because of the risk of bloat, an often fatal condition common in large-chested dogs (see page 164). Bronco's daily diet consisted of breakfast (dry food, usually Eukanuba), lunch (a peanut butter sandwich), dinner (dry food), and one or more Greenies

---

[*] Madeline Lusby, *Leonberger: A Comprehensive Owner's Guide* (Allenhurst, NJ: Kennel Club Books, 2005), 66.

[†] Bronco enjoyed GravyBones, a Milk-Bone product: https://www.milkbone.com/dog-treats/biscuits/gravy-bones.

[‡] Suzanne Dijak-Robinson, "How and Why to Feed Tripe," My Pet Carnivore, October 20, 2017, at https://www.mypetcarnivore.com/how-and-why-to-feed-tripe/.

(dental chews) before bed. The Greenies helped keep his teeth in good condition.

Always ask your veterinarian before making food choices for your dog, but I've found that the foods in the list below make excellent Leonberger snacks.

- Peanut butter
- Apples without the seeds
- Bananas
- Yogurt
- Oatmeal
- Berries
- Carrots
- Cooked eggs
- Cooked fish, especially salmon
- Melon
- Beef jerky
- Cheese

Some substances, including those in the list below, are toxic to dogs.

- Chocolate
- Coffee and caffeine
- Yeast and bread dough containing yeast
- Avocados
- Grapes
- Raisins
- Macadamia nuts
- Fruit pits and seeds
- Raw salmon and trout

- Raw eggs (because of the risk of salmonella)
- Mushrooms
- Garlic
- Onions
- Persimmons
- Rhubarb leaves
- Potato peelings
- Tomatoes
- Tylenol
- Any food or over-the-counter medicine containing the sugar substitute xylitol[*]

Cooked bones are also risky because they can easily splinter into sharp pieces. Also watch out for fish bones: you don't want a fish bone stuck in your dog's throat.

At one point when Bronco was sick, he wouldn't take his medicine, even if we hid it in pill pockets or peanut butter. But he would take it if we tucked it into the middle of a meatball. If you try this trick, be aware that the prepared meatballs you buy at the store typically contain small amounts of onion. The best choice is to make your own meatballs, without the onion.

Also be aware that feeding your dog from the dinner table or kitchen counter increases the risk of weight gain. If you can't feel your dog's ribs under the fat, or if you can't see his waistline, then he is overweight. Frequent weighing will tell you what's going on. Bronco loved getting weighed and would stand on the scale at the veterinarian's office of his own accord, possibly because he knew a treat from the pet store would follow.

[*] Jessica Vogelsang, DVM, "What People Foods Are Harmful to My Pet?," PetMD.com, updated January 20, 2021, at https://www.petmd.com/dog/care/what-people-foods-are-harmful-my-pet.

The Day Bronco, Wearing a Leg Cast, Chased Our Neighbor

When Bronco was almost eight years old, we discovered a case of squamous cell carcinoma in one of his toes—or, rather, in one of his toenails. It was on his right rear paw.

Squamous cell carcinoma is a type of skin cancer that certain large-breed dogs, including Leonbergers, are susceptible to. It often grows out from the skin around the nail and can affect the bone and tissue around it. It is typically not very aggressive, but it can spread, and it is painful. It manifests itself as a swollen toe, or you may be able to see a large red papule that looks like a pimple. Sometimes the toenail falls off. The dog is likely to limp and lick the toe and may become reluctant to go for walks, although that was never the case with Bronco.

Primarily because of the pain, but also because of the small risk of metastasis, it is usually recommended that the affected toe be amputated. So we went through with the procedure.

When we picked Bronco up the day after the surgery, his paw was in a bandage. But he got some treats, and he was in a good mood. We went back to the veterinary surgical center for a bandage change a few times, and then he was done.

Unfortunately, though, we discovered another lesion a year later. This time it was on a large toe on his left front leg. We asked the doctors if the cancer had spread to this toe. We were told no—Bronco was just prone to getting this type of cancer. But the cause could also have been something in the environment. In Texas, the ultraviolet radiation from the sun is significant. We really don't know why this happened to him, but we were assured that it was not because the cancer had spread.

This time around, Bronco's entire leg was put in a cast, to be replaced by a bandage after ten days. We were instructed to keep him inside during those ten days and keep him as still as possible. We were to make sure he wouldn't bump the cast. This was, of course, almost impossible to do, but we were going to try.

However, Bronco really wanted to go out, which he showed us in various ways, such as scratching at the front door. After a week or so, Claudia suggested that we take him outside a little bit, just in our driveway. I agreed. When I handed her the leash, she said, "He can

An agitated Bronco stands guard at the back door. Note the missing toe on his left front paw.

barely walk; do you think he's going to run off without it?" We laughed, and I agreed that it didn't seem like we needed it this time. So Claudia walked out with Bronco slowly limping beside her.

Less than a minute had passed when I heard shouting outside. I opened the door and looked outside to see what was going on. First I saw our neighbor and his two corgis running down the street as fast as they could. Our neighbor was screaming at the top of his lungs, "Get him off me! Get him off me!" Behind him, Bronco was running with his cast going kabonk-kabonk-kabonk as it hit the sidewalk. Behind Bronco ran Claudia, who was also screaming at the top of her lungs. "Bronco! Sit! Stay! Stop!" Finally, Bronco stopped, and Claudia grabbed him. Holding his collar, she led him back in.

Our red-faced and sweaty neighbor was very nice about it and forgave us. He even forgave Bronco, though Bronco was chasing the corgis, not our neighbor. But still, if I had been chased by a big dog wearing a cast, I would not have gotten over it that easily. Our neighbor is clearly a better man than I am.

This was an embarrassing event for all of us, but at the same time it was one of the most surreal and amazing things I've ever seen. It was so unexpected, so bizarre, and so funny. I really wish I had had a video camera handy. Talk about a potentially viral video.

When we went back to the veterinary surgical center to have Bronco's cast removed, we decided not to say anything about the incident to the doctors. We sat in the waiting room and wondered if the episode had caused any permanent damage to Bronco's paw or leg. But when the veterinary technicians came back with Bronco in a bandage instead of a cast, they told us that everything looked good. Great job, everyone!

We thought they might not have checked his sore carefully enough, so we asked them again: Are you sure everything looks good? The sore, the stitches—did you really look at them thoroughly? They insisted that yes, they looked good. So Bronco got his treats, he looked happy, and we went home.

Unfortunately, Bronco would get squamous cell carcinoma on his toes three more times. In two cases, we had the afflicted toe amputated, but in one case we didn't. One reason is that the tumor was growing very slowly, and it seemed to stop bothering him soon after it appeared. Also, it affected the second large toe on his front left leg. It may have become difficult for him to walk if he had had both large toes amputated.

Each time Bronco had toe surgery, he needed to wear a so-called cone of shame to prevent him from licking the site of the amputation. In the beginning, we used a standard hard plastic see-through cone. They are very practical and work well, but they don't seem comfortable. Then we tried a Comfy Cone and a pillow cone. A Comfy Cone is shaped like a standard cone of shame, but it's made

When Bronco wore his Comfy Cone, he sometimes accidentally cleared the coffee table as he walked by.

of a soft material that's comfortable to lean your head on. A pillow cone is an inflatable ring-shaped pillow that you put around a dog's neck. In terms of comfort, this was probably the best solution. But in Bronco's case, it wasn't practical. He was just too big, and he could reach around even the largest size available. For him the best solution was the Comfy Cone.

One More Scare

When he was eleven years old, Bronco was affected by something even more dangerous than squamous cell carcinoma.

After a visit to the groomer, we found that he could no longer stand up on his own. Claudia rushed him to the veterinarian, who gave her

---

Heatstroke

Dogs are much more susceptible to heatstroke than humans, and Leonbergers are more susceptible to heatstroke than most dogs because of their stocky bodies and thick coats. Heatstroke can happen in as little as fifteen minutes.* Don't leave your Leonberger in a car. Avoid strenuous activity on hot days, and exercise your Leonberger early in the morning or late in the evening. If you live in a hot climate, watch out for hot sidewalks, roads, and sandy beaches. Feel the surface with your fingers: Does it feel hot? Does it burn? If so, don't let your dog walk on it. Keep your Leonberger in an air-conditioned dwelling as much as possible and provide plenty of water, shade, and maybe a kiddie pool when he's outside. If there are signs that your Leonberger is getting overheated, you need to cool him off as soon as possible. Ideally, immerse him in cool water and hold his head above the surface to prevent drowning. Alternatively, move him into an air-conditioned building and put cool wet towels or ice packs on his stomach, neck, inner legs, and armpits.

* Laura Playforth, "What Are the Signs of Heat Stroke in Dogs and How Can I Prevent It?," VetsNow, updated April 20, 2021, at https://www.vets-now.com/pet-care-advice/heatstroke-in-dogs/.

a preliminary diagnosis: heatstroke. This diagnosis was later confirmed by lab tests.

Fortunately, treatment started right away, and he slowly recovered. After a couple of days, he was back home, and after a couple of weeks, he could stand up by himself, walk, and run again. But the recovery was difficult. We had never seen him so miserable, and defecating was an issue. Bronco wanted to do it by going outside and squatting, as he usually did. So we used a sling, and I took him out in the morning before I went to work. Claudia's father, Jack, and friend Erica helped her with Bronco during the day.

We didn't complain to the groomer, and we didn't try to investigate the issue. We just never patronized that groomer again. We were simply happy that Bronco recovered and was back to normal.

INTERMEZZO

Ryu Passes

Ryu did not live as long as we had hoped. The typical life span of a Japanese Chin is between twelve and fourteen years. But when he was almost ten years old, Ryu was diagnosed with a growth in his liver. It made him increasingly sick and sapped his energy. The location of the growth made surgery difficult and risky, so we decided not to have it done.

My work had sent me on a monthlong out-of-state assignment, so Claudia had to deal with the situation by herself. One day Ryu had a big seizure, and after talking with our veterinarian, who told us that the prognosis was not good and that putting him down was the best

Toward the end of his life, Ryu was often tired and needed his rest.

we could do for him, we made the decision to euthanize him. Our veterinarian is extremely experienced and on top of things, and we feel blessed to have her.

Losing a dog is always very difficult, and we still miss Ryu years later. We miss his cute, innocent face; his singing; his pep; his cheerful antics. Bronco and Daisy also missed him—or at least we thought they did, based on their behavior. Of course they could have been picking up on our sadness, but they seemed to notice the fact that Ryu was no longer around. For example, on several occasions, when

Little fur angel at the Rainbow Bridge, we will always love you. Run and play, little one.

Intermezzo: Ryu Passes

we spoke about Ryu, Daisy froze, turned around, and looked at us with her big eyes, as if she wanted to ask us something. Her eyes seemed to say, "Where is he?" She did this even six months after his passing.

Bronco missed Ryu as well. Ryu was his little friend. One day when Bronco and I were out walking, we saw a small black-and-white dog in the distance. The dog looked just like Ryu, although I couldn't be sure if he was a Japanese Chin. Bronco stopped his sniffing and looked up. Then he started approaching the dog. As the dog walked off with his owner in a different direction, Bronco stood still and looked at them. I wondered what was going through his mind. I told him, "That's not Ryu, Bronco."

CHAPTER 9

Rollo Rolls In

Six months after Ryu's passing, we decided to get another dog. Rachel really wanted a miniature Australian shepherd, so we got one from a breeder in East Texas. We named him Rollo, after the Viking who was the first ruler of Normandy. In 885–86 CE, Rollo led the Viking siege of Paris but was fended off by Odo, the count of Paris. Our Rollo may not have been quite as brave as the medieval Rollo (or Odo), but he was cute and full of energy.

Rollo was not a big puppy, and at the beginning he was afraid of everything and everyone. However, he quickly warmed up to both Daisy and Bronco, and he was potty trained quickly. Rachel was the one who did most of the training: she stayed with him at night and put a bell on the door to the backyard, which he rang whenever he wanted to go outside. Every time he went, he got a little treat and praise afterward. It made him happy and proud.

We also tried to take him for walks, but he did not understand the concept right away. He would lie down on his back or stand on his hind legs and stretch his paws up, wanting to be carried. So we held him in our arms as we walked him around the neighborhood with

None of us could resist Rollo when he was a young pup.

the other dogs. He was happy up there in our arms, and he contentedly chewed on his leash and harness.

But even after he started walking on his own four feet, he was still a bit anxious and easily frightened. If we saw a cat, we had to turn around and walk straight back home. If we heard a truck engine-braking on the main road a quarter mile away, we had to turn around and walk straight back home. If we saw a man with a little dog, we had to turn around and walk straight back home. If we heard a duck quacking, we had to run for our lives back home. Ducks make strange sounds that can be very scary to little puppies. Whenever we walked or ran back home, I was right behind him as he pulled the leash.

There was one thing Rollo was not afraid of, and that was Bronco. Bronco was the biggest dog Rollo had ever seen—not to mention the biggest dog many people had ever seen—yet Rollo was continually testing Bronco's patience. One time Rollo and I were sitting on the sofa, and Bronco was sleeping at our feet. Suddenly I saw Rollo stepping off the sofa and onto Bronco's back, then walking across Bronco's back down to the floor. Bronco was grumbling a bit, but he let Rollo literally walk all over him.

I also noticed that Rollo liked to play with Bronco's tail. One day Bronco began barking at me intently, as he did when he wanted me to do something or pay attention to him. I couldn't see anything amiss at first, but then I saw something going on behind him. I took a closer look and saw Rollo dangling from Bronco's tail. He was bit-

"Please, Bronco, I want my belly rub."

Rollo Rolls In

To my astonishment, Bronco didn't react angrily when Rollo swung like Tarzan from his tail.

ing it and using it as a swing. I got Rollo off right away, of course, which is exactly what Bronco wanted. He was being very patient with Rollo, but Rollo wanted to play.

Of course, the dogs often go in the backyard to do their business (I don't mean the kind of business that's taxable). This requires me to do pickup duty. On one occasion I was walking up and down the lawn, looking for poop and picking it up, when Rollo ran over to my left side and pushed me with his nose and nipped my shoes a little bit. Then he ran behind me and did the same thing on my right side. Then he ran behind me again and repeated the process, and so it went—over and over and over. Then I realized that to him, I was a sheep, and he was having fun herding me. He herded me down the lawn and back up again until all the poop was picked up. We were a team: he the herding dog in charge and I the pooper-picker-upper sheep. We performed this ritual several times. Claudia and I thought about taking him to one of those farms where you can let your shepherd dog herd sheep just for fun, but we never got around to it.

Rollo soon found something else he seemed to enjoy even more, and that was playing with balls—chasing them, fetching them, chewing them, pushing them, rolling them, kicking them, jumping on them, and biting them. It is a truly amazing sight. There's so much energy and joie de vivre involved. To this day, whenever a ball rolls under a sofa, Rollo gets upset and barks at the sofa. Then you have to bend down and get the ball out. You better do what he wants or he'll wail like a toddler.

Rollo also loved chewing on shoes when he was younger. Fortunately, he's gotten over that behavior, but in the process we've lost a lot of shoes. One time I forgot that I had left my shoes under a table in our TV room. I was walking around the house when I met Rollo in a hallway holding one of my shoes in his mouth. He gave me a deer-in-the-headlights look, then he slowly turned around and tiptoed back into the TV room. He placed my shoe back under the table, right next to its mate, positioning it correctly so it was just the way I had left it. Then he tiptoed away as if pretending that nothing had happened.

Rollo could be quite an artist when it came to shoes. Maybe we should have framed his work instead of throwing it away. Maybe we should have established a little chewed-shoe museum so people could have paid admission to see it.

Rollo is also pretty good at finding weird things in the backyard and bringing them into the house—snails, lizards, strange-looking

Rollo plays with one of his favorite toys.

The artist poses with one of his creations.

larvae and worms, caterpillars, and creatures that might have been space aliens. I'm not sure: I mean, I've seen *Men in Black*, and some of the stuff he brought in could have been small versions of the creatures from that movie. Our backyard looks like a typical backyard on the surface, but Rollo made us realize that it's actually an amazing world full of amazing creatures.

One day as I was walking Daisy and Rollo, we saw a frog, or perhaps it was a toad. It was jumping ahead of us. Both Daisy and Rollo had been looking down, sniffing the asphalt and the grass. As the frog jumped in front of us, the dogs became very curious. They sniffed and looked closely at the frog, and then, for the first time, Rollo looked up at me, straight into my eyes, questioning. *What is that?* I got the strange feeling that he wanted me to explain.

I told Rollo, "It's a frog." Even though he doesn't understand English—or at least I don't think he does—it seemed like he wanted

Canis lupus, the gray wolf, is a fearsome and courageous hunter in nature.

Canis lupus familiaris, the dog—a close relative of the gray wolf—is sometimes less brave. This specimen prefers to sit in a stroller when he hears strange sounds.

me to say more, give him some indication that this unfamiliar life form wasn't dangerous. Then Rollo gently touched the frog with his paw and patted it a bit. He was enjoying himself, but the frog may have felt differently. The world is full of wonders when you're a puppy.

It's also full of things that can seem threatening. So even though we got a stroller for Daisy, the dog who I think uses it the most is Rollo—although not because he gets tired walking. On the contrary, he seems to have endless energy. But Rollo is a bit of an anxious dog, and he feels safe in the stroller.

Bronco, Protector of Small Dogs

I believe dogs have empathy, and sometimes they want to share—at least Bronco did. There was a time when we were in our home eating take-out food and Bronco stole one of our dinners, including meat, vegetables, and a baked potato. He started eating the meat, then he glanced at Daisy, who was sitting in the middle of the floor looking sad. Immediately he took the baked potato in his mouth and carried it over to her and dropped it right at her feet. I was going to get mad at him for stealing, but when I saw his kindhearted and unselfish act, I let it be.

On another occasion, Bronco did something else amazing for Daisy. Despite having issues with his paws—this was around the time he was being treated for squamous cell carcinoma—he saved Daisy from an attacking German shepherd who was running loose.

We were at Claudia's parents' house, just leaving, when one of their neighbors came out to drop some garbage in the trash can at the end of her driveway. With her was a young, probably adolescent, German shepherd, and he was not on a leash. As we were standing on the porch, I suddenly saw the shepherd flying through the bushes, his teeth bared. He quickly charged us—viciously.

Just as Rachel protects Rollo and Daisy, Bronco protected the smaller dogs, sometimes at his own peril.

First he went for Daisy, but Bronco got between them to protect her. Essentially, Bronco saved her life. The shepherd bit his leg in return. Bronco was almost twelve when this happened, and he was not as strong as he used to be. A German shepherd would have been an easy opponent for Bronco just a few years earlier, but at that point he was old, and he did not need the extra stress.

I kicked the German shepherd in the stomach, and he ran off. Bronco's legs were weak—he had recently had one of his toe operations, and his walking was unsteady—so seeing the shepherd going for the leg on which he had had his operation was very upsetting. The shepherd could have bitten me, of course, and I could have been severely injured, but I didn't care. I was defending my dogs—who were all on a leash, by the way. If the shepherd had bitten me, the owner could have been criminally charged, and there could have been a lawsuit.

The owner of the shepherd came over to apologize, but I cursed at her. Maybe I shouldn't have, but she had a vicious and dangerous dog, and she intentionally let him run loose. In the end, though, there were no major injuries. Bronco's leg was slightly hurt, but overall, he was fine. These days, whenever we talk about this incident, I jokingly refer to the neighbor dog as Cujo.

When Dogs Speak

Remember the old joke about the man who heard a woman speak to her cat as if the cat understood her? He thought it was so funny that he went home and told his dogs about it, and they laughed and laughed.

It reminds me of what happened when we visited a car dealership with Bronco. The salesman told us a story about a woman who kept talking to her dog as if he were a person. He was laughing and told us that she was probably crazy. He put his finger to his temple and twirled it in circles to underscore his point. But we didn't think his story was funny. I mean, what dog owner doesn't talk to her dogs?

In fact, that day at the dealership, we let Bronco walk in and out of the various cars we were considering and sit in the back seats. The salesman didn't mind. He was the one who suggested it! You can say that in practice, it was Bronco who chose the car we bought.

Bronco was a little bit of a commando. He unfailingly let us know when it was 5:00 p.m.—time for dinner. His stomach operated like clockwork. He also told us when he wanted to be petted, when he wanted to go for a walk, and when something was wrong. When he wanted a treat, he walked straight up to you and stared you in the face. He didn't bark; he just gave you that intense "Please give me a treat" stare that you couldn't say no to. When something was wrong, he barked slowly but loudly while looking at you. The other dogs started doing the same thing. Maybe they learned it from Bronco, or maybe it's inherent dog behavior. That doesn't mean that Bronco was domineering or thought he was in charge. But like a confident and secure child, he was not afraid to ask for what he wanted.

Rollo is much the same way. When he wants to jump up on the sofa, he scratches it with his paw so you know you need to move over. When he can't find his favorite toy, he'll tell you, and you have to find it for him. When he wants to go to bed, he barks at the bed so that you'll lie down beside him. That's all fine, as long as you let your dogs know who's in charge.

Another thing that dogs seem to be very vocal about is their responsibility to guard the front door. Whenever they hear a doorbell, an alarm on a smartphone connected to a home-security camera, or an old-fashioned knock, they have to tell everyone about it.

Have you ever been played by a dog? Well, we were played by our dogs. We aren't proud of it, but it was a learning experience. It happened like this: sometimes when the dogs heard the neighbor's dog barking through the open back door, they ran outside to bark back at him. We didn't want them to disturb the entire neighborhood, so we called them inside again. Unfortunately, they would sometimes ignore us. So foolishly, we started bribing them with little treats. Each time they came back inside, they would get one.

Maybe you can guess what happened next. The dogs started running outside to bark several times a day, even when the neighbor's dog wasn't there. In fact, their efforts to bark became halfhearted, and they didn't even run all the way to the fence. They figured out that being called back inside resulted in treats if they complied, so why not make sure they got called back by running out? They got their treats for a while until we put an end to it.

One thing I realized about dogs is that they don't hide their feelings. They don't try to explain the special theory of relativity to you

Rollo Rolls In

or express their opinion on the bouquet of the beer they're drinking. They are direct and uncomplicated: "I want this"; "I feel this"; and you can trust what they're saying. Well, maybe there's some minor trickery at work when they want a treat, but except for *that* you can trust what dogs are telling you. In that sense they have a lot in common with a young child. A young child expresses his feelings with his facial expressions, or by crying, or by banging his spoon. Dogs are direct in the same way. That's a big part of why we love them and why we trust them. Dogs have integrity.

When Rollo was in his playpen, we were sure he would be safe in case Bronco decided he had had enough of his younger sibling's antics.

Baby Jail or Private Puppy Residence?

Rollo often pushed his luck with Bronco—climbing all over him, sitting on him, and stealing his possessions. Bronco was very patient and protective of little Rollo, but we were afraid he would lose patience with him one day when we were not present. Therefore, we put Rollo in a playpen whenever we left the house.

The playpen had a door that swung open and could be locked. Soon he learned to go through the door on his own when we asked him to. We would say, "Rollo, playpen," and he would march right in. We made sure that the playpen contained water and toys and that the door was locked behind him. Of course, we didn't leave him there too long. Experts recommend a maximum of two hours when the puppy is two months old and a maximum of three hours when the puppy is three months old. Even when Rollo was older than that, we never left him in the playpen longer than four hours.

Rollo's relationship with his playpen was interesting. When Daisy tried to walk in, Rollo would get angry. The playpen was Rollo's, and no one else could enter. It was his little house within a house. Sometimes he would walk in even if we didn't ask him to, and he would just sit there for a while, as if he needed some alone time.

David's girlfriend, Meranda, came up with a great name for Rollo's playpen: baby jail. So that's what we called it, and Rollo seemed to like it. When we told Rollo, "Rollo, baby jail," he would march right in, just as he did when we called it a playpen. Even though he didn't seem to mind it, he was always eager to come back out when we got home. He would stand on his hind legs, jump up and down, and bark. Then we would rush to greet him and lift him out of his baby jail.

CHAPTER 10

Black October and the Grey Muzzle Award

October of 2019 was a very difficult month for Bronco. He was getting old, and he had the first signs of geriatric-onset laryngeal paralysis polyneuropathy (or GOLPP; see page 167), which made his breathing a bit labored and affected his gait. In addition, he had developed another case of squamous cell carcinoma, this time on his right rear paw, and that toe was amputated on October 3—the day he turned twelve years and three months old. The surgery went well, but after around ten days it was discovered that he had a large deep ulcerous sore on the same paw a few inches above the surgical scar. Fortunately, it was not cancerous, as we first thought, but we would have to treat this sore in addition to nursing him back from his amputation.

On October 20, I was sitting in our backyard. Claudia and the dogs were inside. I was finished walking the dogs, and the sun had just set. A severe thunderstorm was approaching, and there was a tornado watch in effect—but that's not unusual for North Texas. I was sipping a delicious Texas beer, an IPA called Yellow Rose, when my cell phone started beeping. It was a tornado warning—upgraded from a tornado watch. I also heard tornado sirens, but they weren't very loud, and as I found out later, some people didn't hear them at all.

About the same time as I heard the sirens, I saw lightning in the distance and heard thunder. I decided to finish my beer and go inside to be safe. A few minutes after I walked in, it started raining heavily, and the wind became very rough. It sounded like golf-ball-size hail was hitting the roof. The house shook from the winds, then suddenly there was a loud boom.

I thought lightning had struck the house. What I didn't know was that a flying block of concrete had just smashed our chimney. Bronco was calm, and the little dogs seemed okay, too.

After the wind had died down a bit, I opened the door to the backyard, and what I saw shocked me. My gas grill had flown across the patio. There were bricks and pieces of concrete all over the patio and the lawn. There was a big sheet of metal lying on the patio. Big tree branches covered the lawn. There was debris everywhere. We had also lost power. I didn't notice until the next morning that our chimney had been smashed and that the roof was covered in bricks and debris. It turns out that an EF3 tornado had gone through our neighborhood and passed within fifty to one hundred yards of our house.

Claudia called her parents, who live only a mile from us. They had been badly hit, but they seemed fine on the phone, and they didn't complain. Still, she asked me to drive over and check on them. But as soon as I turned out of our driveway, I saw my neighbor's roof lying on the street, rendering it impassable. I turned around and tried to go the other way, but that didn't work, either. Across that end of the road lay a huge pile of trees.

So I parked the car in my driveway and started to walk toward their house. I was stopped by four firemen, who told me that it was

The damage to my neighbor's house after the tornado of October 2019 was devastating. Her roof lay across the street.

not safe to walk around the neighborhood. They asked me to go back home.

It was dark, but I could see some of the carnage. I realized that we had been lucky. Many of our neighbors had lost their entire homes. We ended up needing a new chimney, a new roof, a new fence, and a few other things, but we were fine.

The damage to Claudia's parents' house was more severe, which we would discover the next day when we visited them. Their windows had been blown in, and Claudia's dad had to hold on to a doorframe in order to keep himself from being carried away. A broken marble tabletop hit him in the back and gave him a foot-long bruise. He did not go to the hospital.

The Preston Royal shopping center was also devastated by the tornado. That's where our veterinarian's office was located. Thank good-

Bronco, who was not at his best in this picture, rests next to our tornado-damaged fence. We put a plastic bag around his bandage when he went outside.

ness they didn't have any animals staying overnight that night, but the clinic was gone. So were many stores and restaurants. Our favorite supermarket was destroyed. The school our boys went to was severely damaged, and some buildings were later torn down. There was debris all over the neighborhood.

Claudia's parents had to move out of their house while repairs were made, but although we were able to stay in our house, we didn't have power for four days. There was no cell-phone signal in our neighborhood. The streets weren't navigable, so I couldn't go to work. It was also hot, so this was stressful for Bronco.

A Serious Condition

We don't know if the heat had anything to do with it, but about a week after the tornado, Bronco developed congestive heart failure.

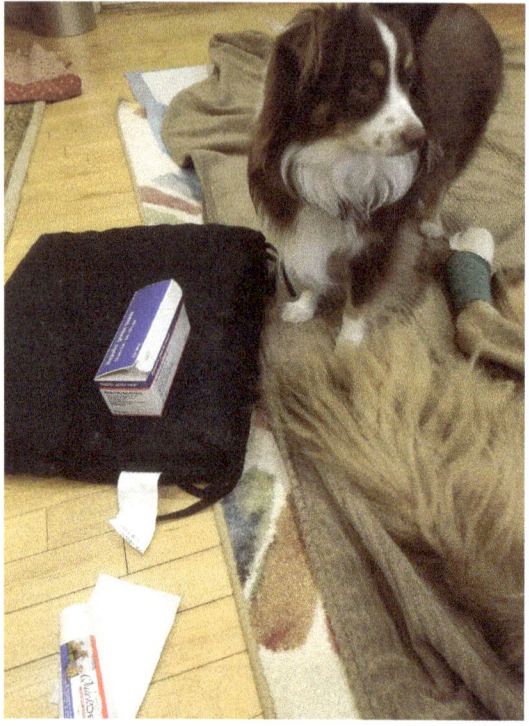

Rollo helps change one of Bronco's bandages.

As a result, he could no longer walk. The veterinary cardiologist at the surgical center told us that Bronco was not in good shape, but we all agreed that we should give him a chance to recover.

We bought Help 'Em Up harnesses for him, but more often we used a smaller sling to help him stand up. We also treated his heart with various medications. Since our veterinarian's office had been destroyed, we took him to the veterinary surgical center (where he had his toe amputated) for bandage changes. After a few visits, the technicians suggested that we do it at home to save time and money. More important, it would be easier on Bronco. So they gave us instructions, and we started doing it at home.

But changing Bronco's bandages wasn't as easy as just rolling out some gauze and tape. First we had to clean the sores with chlorhexidine, an antiseptic solution. Then we had to apply a healing ointment, such as manuka honey or QuickDerm. This involved spreading it on an Adaptic pad (breathable and nonstick), then wrapping the pad with a Telfa pad (or gauze pad). After that came the soft bandage, then the outer bandage, then something sticky to hold it all together. The latter was necessary because bandages easily slip off dog hair.

I did most of the bandage changes, but Claudia and the children helped, and even Rollo helped. He was very curious: he stood by and watched everything I did as if he were checking to see that I didn't forget anything. He loved Bronco's bandage changes and seemed to think that they were very interesting. It was never a problem—except for the time he drank the chlorhexidine.[*]

During this period, we gave Bronco a lot of attention. We slept next to him at night and petted him a lot. He needed help to get up, and we were ready to do that at any time. Sometimes he just wanted to walk around. Sometimes he wanted water, and sometimes he wanted to go out in the backyard to pee or just lie in the grass.

In the beginning it was Claudia who did most of the caretaking. But I took early retirement in November, and I started taking over the night duty. Bronco came to expect constant company, which was okay with us, even though at times it was very tiring. For example, if I was petting him and stopped doing so, he would whine or bark and essentially order me to continue.

At the same time, taking care of him was an amazing experience for me. Bronco usually slept on his dog bed next to the sofa, and I slept on the sofa next to him. When he wanted something, he sat up and looked at me. He did not make a sound. I would wake up, prob-

---

[*] We called our veterinarian's office, and the technicians told us that the chlorhexidine was probably not harmful to Rollo. Chlorhexidine is a type of salt, and unless it's ingested in large quantities, it's nontoxic—unlike peroxide.

ably because I could feel him staring at me. I would open my eyes, and there would be Bronco's big beautiful face looking down at me, his gentle expression asking for help. I would get up and help him with whatever he needed.

Bronco was able to communicate what he wanted just by looking at me. It felt like I could understand what he was thinking and feel-

You can see how happy Bronco was to be outside, even as his health was not the best.

ing even though he couldn't speak. It almost felt as if he were becoming an extension of me, or maybe the other way around—I was becoming an extension of him. We were two very close buddies who understood each other. They say that a dog is man's best friend, but for us it was not just a cute cliché. We *were* best friends.

The veterinarians advised us not to take Bronco out for walks until he was in better condition. But one day he lay at the front door, scratching it and whining. I could clearly see that he wanted to go out. So I took him on a very slow walk. We walked, then he rested; he sniffed his surroundings, and I brought water for him to drink. Along the way we met a woman who looked him and said, "What a beautiful dog." You can see in the photo on page 120, taken during that walk, that he was old and tired, but he was still beautiful.

This warmed my heart. The woman asked what kind of dog he was, and she appeared to be really interested and impressed. It was the first time Bronco had been out walking in perhaps a month, and after all we'd been through, I have to admit I needed the experience, and Bronco did, too. After that, we started taking short walks every now and then, and when we were finished, Claudia would pick us up in the car.

After a while, Bronco was able to get around on his own and even go to the bathroom on his own, and his sore got closer to healing. In fact, he recovered almost miraculously. We were extremely happy about this, and it made everyone's lives easier.

We had been planning a big family vacation for several months, which Claudia and I had considered canceling. It was a one-week cruise along the Mississippi River, and it was scheduled for December of 2019. Because of Bronco's improvement, we decided to go. But we had learned our lesson: while we were gone, a friend of ours lived in our house and watched our dogs. We showed her how to change Bronco's bandage, and that arrangement worked out well.

Bronco had a tough October followed by a difficult but successful recovery. Taking into account his other health scares—including heatstroke and the freak accident with the metal rod when he was young—our veterinarian told us that Bronco must have nine lives, like a cat.

Bronco's Grey Muzzle Award

A happy event that took place a few weeks after our Mississippi River trip was that Bronco received an award for longevity: the Grey Muzzle Award, given by the Leonberger Health Foundation International, which bestows the award on any Leonberger who has reached the age of twelve.[*] The Grey Muzzle Award is also given to breeders, because they are partially responsible for the dogs' longevity. It was a happy time in the Wikman family.

These Leonbergers are the canine equivalents of centenarians—humans who are at least one hundred years old. You don't have to have your Leonberger registered with the LCA or AKC to apply for the award—it's open to all purebred Leonbergers around the world. You can also apply if your dog is deceased, as long as he lived past the age of twelve. Incidentally, the oldest Leonberger on record is Su-Riya (formally Genette of Mutsugoro), who lived in Japan and died in 2017 at the ripe old age of sixteen years and three months.

If you have a twelve-year-old Leonberger, simply fill out a form on the LHFI website or send an email to lhfgreymuzzle@gmail.com. The foundation will ask for some information, including the registered name and call name of the dog; the breeder's name, kennel name, address, and email; the dam's registered name; the sire's

---

[*] For more information, see https://www.lhfi.org/the-grey-muzzle-award.html; to see the 2019–2020 awardees, including Bronco, visit https://youtu.be/qS9w6Zk1Hz4.

The Leonberger Health Foundation International
106 La Sonoma Way • Alamo, CA 94507

February 19, 2020

Dear Thomas & Claudia,

On behalf of the Leonberger Health Foundation International we wish to congratulate you for providing a wonderful, healthful home for Le Bronco von der Löwenhöle, "Bronco."

Bronco will be featured at the 2020 Leonberger Club of America's National Club Show awards banquet and appeared in the January 2020 edition of the *LeoLetter*.

Throughout the world only a small handful of our wonderful Leonbergers reach the age of 12 years. Thank you for helping to set a standard for longevity we hope more and more Leonbergers will achieve in the coming years.

The Leonberger Health Foundation International has made Leonberger longevity a priority. We have raised from generous donations of LeoLovers over $300,000.00, and have distributed that money to scientific researchers in the United States and Europe who are devoting their lives to finding and eliminating diseases like LPN, Addisons, cancers and cardiac disorders in Leonbergers. An increase in breed longevity will be a strong indicator of our success.

Amanda Thiessen
for the
Grey Muzzle Team

The Grey Muzzle Award

FOR LEONBERGER LONGEVITY
IS PRESENTED WITH GRATITUDE
BY
THE LEONBERGER HEALTH
FOUNDATION INTERNATIONAL
TO

Bronco

FOR OFFERING HOPE AND
POTENTIAL FOR
LONGER LIVES FOR LEONBERGERS
THROUGHOUT THE
WORLD

2020

registered name; the owner's name, address, and email; the birth date of the dog; and whether the dog is alive or dead. If the latter, they will want to know the cause of death. In addition, they would like you to write a one-paragraph tribute to the dog and send two (preferably high-resolution) photos—one head shot and one favorite photo.

I found out about the Grey Muzzle award via a Facebook group called the Leonberger Double Digit Club. We applied for the award a little bit late, but we received it in February of 2020, when Bronco was twelve years and seven months old. At the time, he had recovered from his collapse the previous October and was doing pretty well. He was subsequently mentioned at the LCA's awards banquet and featured in a video about long-lived Leonbergers produced by the LHFI.

I would encourage anyone who owns a Leonberger who is at least ten years old to join the Facebook Leonberger Double Digit Club. There you can gather a tremendous amount of information and helpful tips. Its members share photos and stories and advice for dealing with old-age problems, food issues, and more.

INTERMEZZO

The Last Car Ride

During May and June of 2020, Bronco's geriatric-onset laryngeal paralysis polyneuropathy worsened. His breathing became labored, and he had a much harder time walking, even with help. He tried to relieve himself in the backyard, and sometimes that worked, but at other times he couldn't help but go inside the house. We didn't mind this too much. We cleaned it up, then we cleaned him up and tried to comfort him. However, we could see that he was embarrassed about

Death leaves a heartache no one can heal,

But love leaves a memory no one can steal.

the situation. Claudia's sister Isabella gave us a shampoo machine that made it easier and quicker to clean him up if necessary. Bronco quickly got used to the machine and the massaging feel it had. We also tried to take him for a few short walks, which he seemed to enjoy even though we didn't get very far. I slept next to him every night, and Claudia stayed next to him during the day. He always had someone by his side. We gave him chicken-bouillon ice cubes to cool his throat, which also helped his breathing. And we made sure the house was kept cool.

In addition to the laryngeal paralysis, which is incurable, other issues had started to resurface, including his heart. The one cancerous toe that we did not have amputated was also starting to flare up. He probably had arthritis, and he was very old for a Leonberger. It seemed like the time had come for him to be put to sleep.

This is an extremely difficult decision for any dog owner. How do you ascertain your dog's quality of life and prospects for recovery? How do you balance that with the feeling that he's probably suffering? Facing this reality is heartbreaking, and you will feel sadness and guilt no matter what you do. But it's always better to put a dog to sleep than to let him suffer.

Bronco's thirteenth birthday, on July 3, was approaching, but we agreed that we would not let the date influence our decision.

In the wee hours of the morning on June 16, 2020, Bronco collapsed. He was no longer able to get up or hold himself up even if we lifted him. His legs were like spaghetti, and his breathing was heavy. We called our veterinarian as soon as the clinic opened. She spent quite a bit of time with us over the phone trying to figure out what was going on. The preliminary conclusion was that he most likely was experiencing another episode of heart failure.

We decided—all of us, together with our veterinarian—that it was time. Our veterinarian knew Bronco extremely well: she really cared for him, and she was not afraid to tell us how she felt.

Rachel and I would take Bronco to the clinic, where he would be put to sleep. Claudia would stay at home with the other dogs.

Rachel, Claudia, and I lifted him into the car—all 142 pounds of him. It was the first time he could do nothing to help. But once he was inside the car, he was able to rest his head on the center console, between the armrests of the front seats, and sometimes he lifted his head so that he could see out.

He was exhausted but very curious about what he could see out the windows. We had some extra time before our appointment, so we took him for a car ride instead of driving straight to the clinic. He seemed to enjoy it: he was looking at things that seemed to interest him, but he did not make a sound, and he didn't move much. After a while we turned around and started heading toward the clinic. We dreaded what was coming, but it was time.

Our veterinarian was waiting for us. The staff put Bronco on a stretcher and rolled him inside. Seeing my best friend lying on a stretcher being rolled into a clinic and knowing these were his last moments on earth was surreal. Our veterinarian checked him to verify what was going on. His blood pressure was extremely low, and his heart was not pumping normally. It was indeed heart failure. Rachel was FaceTiming Claudia so she could talk to Bronco. We did everything we could to comfort him.

Our veterinarian and her assistant had taken care of Bronco for around ten years, and we had visited them quite often toward the end of his life. They both knew him really well, and they truly cared for him. The veterinarian had told us that Bronco was the oldest big dog she'd ever treated, and they both said that he had become like family to them; he wasn't just another patient. The situation was upsetting for them, too. Putting him to sleep was not an easy thing for any of us, but it was the right thing to do.

We all petted him, and Rachel and Claudia spoke to him to comfort him. I was not able to say much—it was just too difficult—but I made sure Bronco heard my voice a few times and that he could see me. The room was somber but peaceful and filled with love. First he

Bronco

Bronco von der Lowenhohle
July 3, 2007 to June 16, 2020
Loved by Claudia, Thomas, Jacob, David, Rachel Wikman
Dallas, TX

Our beloved Bronco passed away peacefully last summer two weeks short of thirteen years old. It was sudden but not unexpected. He was old, his heart was failing, and he had other health issues as well. When his second heart failure happened on June 16, we all knew it was time. We were with him all the way to the end, and we said goodbye. He knew, but he was at peace. It was a heart-rending experience for all of us, including the veterinary and her assistant. Bronco had become family to them as well. Our veterinarian said he was the biggest, oldest dog she had ever treated.

When he came into our lives as a happy, rambunctious and confident puppy he instantly stole our hearts. He became the mascot for our daughter's soccer team, and he went to every game. At half time, the girls all lined up to pet him - including the opposing team. He was the main attraction. Each girl got one minute to pet him. He wasn't scared. He loved every minute of it. He grew big quickly, and his size and strength amazed us and everyone in the neighborhood. He loved greeting people and dogs and wanted to say hello to everyone we met on walks. He was not just the greeter in chief at our house but at the dog park as well. He also loved swimming and chasing ducks in White Rock Lake.

Bronco amazed us with his intelligence and abilities so many times. When our hamsters escaped from their cage, my wife tried to enlist Bronco in helping us find them. He understood, and he sniffed them out and found them. This happened twice. We had a Labrador with diabetes called Baylor. One day Bronco alerted us to the fact that something was going on with Baylor. Soon thereafter Baylor had an insulin shock. No one had taught Bronco to detect this, he just did, and it probably helped us get Baylor to the emergency sooner. On another occasion, Bronco saved our Pug Daisy from an attack by a loose German Shepherd. He also chased off a trespasser; Bronco probably just wanted to greet him and lick him, but the intruder didn't know that.

We will never forget Bronco's loving and trusting eyes, his lust for life, his Leonberger hugs when he leaned into us. He was very social, and his love for people and other dogs, especially small dogs, was remarkable. He had an enormous patience for rambunctious small dogs, and he took it upon himself to protect them. At the age of twelve and a half, he got the "grey muzzle award," which was a fun experience for all of us. We think of Bronco every day, and we miss him dearly. He will forever be in our hearts.

Bronco's obituary appeared in the September 2021 issue of LeoLetter, the official publication of the Leonberger Club of America.

got a shot that put him to sleep, and then after he was completely asleep, the veterinarian gave him a drug that stopped his heart. It stopped beating less than fifteen seconds after the injection. Bronco had passed across the Rainbow Bridge. The room was quiet, but human hearts were not.

Bronco was cremated, and we picked up the box containing his remains and his paw print the next day. The veterinarian and her assistant also wrote us a beautiful card that will forever stay with us.

Bronco had a long life and a big heart. He was loving, caring, protective, and brave. So it's almost fitting that heart disease ultimately caused his death. This calls to mind the legend of Sven Dufva, the fictional Finnish hero who was shot in the heart in the Finnish War of 1808–1809. In the epic poem *The Tales of Ensign Stål*, Dufva's commanding general stands over his body and proclaims:

> *That bullet knew what course to take, it must acknowledged be. . . .*
> *It knew far more than we.*
> *It let his brow be spared in peace, the weaker, poorer part,*
> *And chose the portion that was best—his noble, valiant heart.*

CHAPTER 11

History of the Leonberger

The Leonberger breed was originally created by Heinrich Essig (1808–87) in the German town of Leonberg, in what was then the kingdom of Württemberg. According to legend, Essig bred the dog to resemble the lion in the town's coat of arms.* Indeed, as you can see in the image on page 132, the lion in the coat of arms doesn't look like a real lion, so you could say that the Leonberger looks the way it does because Germans were bad at drawing lions back then. All joking aside, though, Leonbergers do bear some resemblance to lions and maybe even bears. In any case, they are beautiful dogs.

When people would stop me and ask me questions about the kind of dog Bronco was, I would say he was a Leonberger—a cross between a Saint Bernard, a Newfoundland, and a Great Pyrenees—and that the breed was created by the mayor of the German town of Leonberg. But, as the economist Tyler Cowen said, "Be suspicious of simple stories." As it turns out, the story I kept telling was a simplifi-

---

* Madeline Lusby, *Leonberger: A Comprehensive Owner's Guide* (Allenhurst, NJ: Kennel Club Books, 2005).

cation and not entirely true. History is more complicated, and that's another reason I'm writing this book: I was unintentionally spreading misinformation about Leonbergers, and want to try to correct some of it.

Simple and interesting stories are easy to remember, easy to believe, and easy to propagate. But first, Heinrich Essig was never the mayor of Leonberg. He was a prominent citizen of the town, and he was a successful businessman, farmer, innkeeper, horse and dog trader, large-dog enthusiast, dog breeder, and town councilman, but he was never the mayor.

Essig claimed to have created the Leonberger in the 1830s by crossing a female Landseer Newfoundland with a male long-haired Saint Bernard from the Great Saint Bernard Hospice, a monastery in Switzerland. He continued crossing the Landseer Newfoundland and the Saint Bernard over four generations, then he crossed his Newfoundland–Saint Bernard mix with a Pyrenean wolfhound—not, as is often asserted, with a Great Pyrenees (called a Pyrenean mountain dog in Europe). He then crossed that dog with the Saint

The coat of arms of the town of Leonberg, Germany, was allegedly the inspiration for the first breeder of the Leonberger, Heinrich Essig.

Bernard again. In 1846, he was finally ready to announce and register his "lion of a dog." A few years later, Leonbergers were officially introduced to the public at the Munich Oktoberfest.*

However, the story is more complicated than that. There's no specific breed named Pyrenean wolfhound today, so Essig could have used a Great Pyrenees or a Pyrenean mastiff. In addition, later in the nineteenth century, Leonbergers were used to breed the long-haired Saint Bernard dog, and this likely saved the Saint Bernard dog from extinction. At one point, too, Leonbergers were deliberately mixed with Newfoundland dogs to strengthen the Newfoundland breed. In other words, breeding happened in both directions, and the characteristics of the large breeds were in constant flux. The dogs—including Leonbergers and Saint Bernards—didn't look like they do today, either. Essig's Leonbergers were multicolored, mostly white, and lacked the black mask that is so important to the breed now. What has not changed is the essence of what Essig was aiming for: a large but moderately proportioned dog that is friendly and loving and a great companion.†

Ultimately, the origins of the Leonberger, as well as the Saint Bernard and the other large breeds from this region, are complex and shrouded in mystery. In addition, some of Essig's claims have been disputed. Breed standards wouldn't be codified until the end of the nineteenth century. It should also be noted that it was Essig's niece Marie who to a large extent bred and cared for the dogs.‡

Essig was selling his Leonberger dogs as luxury items to the wealthy. He was also a marketing genius and was able to get the at-

---

* Lusby, *Leonberger*.
† Caroline Bliss-Isberg, *Leonberger: A Comprehensive Guide to the Lion King of Breeds* (Sea Cliff, NY: Revodana Publishing, 2017), 23, 41, 45, 48–49.
‡ See the Leonberger Union's "The History of the Breed," at https://www.leonbergerunion.com/breed-history.html

tention of European nobility and royalty. The czar of Russia, Emperor Napoleon II, Otto von Bismarck, the king of Belgium, Empress Elisabeth of Austria, Emperor Maximilian I, the Prince of Wales, King Umberto of Italy, Giuseppe Garibaldi, and the mikado of Japan were among those who owned Leonbergers.* Not everyone was happy about this. Some people viewed the Leonberger as a fashionable knockoff of the Saint Bernard that could hinder that breed's development.†

Toward the end of the nineteenth century, the discipline of cynology, or the scientific study of dogs, emerged. Cynologists pushed for breed classification and systematic breeding practices, and breed standards were created. But Essig and others viewed dog breeding as an art rather than a science, and this led to a conflict with the cynologists. Heinrich Schumacher, for example, was a breeder who strove to create a clearly identifiable Saint Bernard type. He was upheld by the cynologists as a paragon, in contrast to Heinrich Essig—to the detriment of the Leonberger.

After Essig's death, in 1887, other people more willing to please the cynologists continued breeding Leonbergers. By that time, the dogs looked for the most part like Leonbergers do today. Then, in 1895, Albert Kull created the Leonberger's first breed standard. It would go through several revisions—in 1901, 1926, 1938, 1951, 1955, and 1972—until finally, in 1996, the FCI‡-approved version was established. The Kennel Club in the UK and the American Kennel Club also have their own breed standards. However, most of them are sim-

---

* Geeske Joel, "Leonberger Breed History," at http://www.leonberger-hunde.org/breed_history.html.
† Joel, "Leonberger Breed History."
‡ The Fédération Cynologique Internationale, or FCI, serves as a kind of worldwide kennel club for all breeds. It was created on May 22, 1911, with the goal of promoting and protecting cynology and purebred dogs. See the federation's website at http://www.fci.be/en/.

ilar to Albert Kull's 1895 version. The first Leonberger club was formed 1891 in Berlin: two more were created in 1895, then two more were formed in 1901. The most prominent was the Internationaler Klub für Leonberger Hunde, of which Albert Kull was the first president.

———

World War I was tough on the breed. Some Leonbergers were used to pull ammunition carts and small cannons during the conflict, and others were left to wander unattended. Often, these dogs starved to death. But after the war, two Leonberg businessmen, Karl Stadelmann and Otto Josenhans, worked hard to save the breed. They scoured the countryside looking for Leonbergers who were still alive. They were able to find twenty-five of them whose owners were willing to cooperate in reestablishing the breed. Of these, only five were suitable for breeding.* None of the Leonberger clubs had survived, so they founded a new one in 1922 called Deutsche Club für Leonberger Hunde (DCLH), and Stadelmann created an updated version of Albert Kull's breed standard.

I've read that World War II was even more devastating to the breed. Supposedly† there were only eight Leonbergers left in the world after the end of the war, and all Leonbergers today are descendants of those eight surviving Leonbergers. That's once again a fascinating and simple story that's easy to remember and spread, but the truth is rarely simple.

The Leonberger, like so many other dog breeds, was devastated by World War II—kennels were destroyed; dogs were left unattended or

---

* Joel, "Leonberger Breed History."
† See the *Wikipedia* entry for the Leonberger as well as George Hoppendale and Asia Moore, *Leonberger: Leonberger Dog Complete Owners Manual* (IMB Publishing, 2015). Also see Lusby, *Leonberger*.

used for food—but Leonbergers weren't used in the war effort itself, and there were more than eight left afterward. However, there was indeed a "genetic bottleneck" of Leonbergers in the 1940s, meaning that the population was greatly reduced in size, limiting the genetic diversity of the species. This was largely because people repeatedly bred the dogs they thought were the best specimens in a misguided attempt to improve the breed. Of course, for breed (and species) health, you need diversity. Scientific pedigree analyses demonstrate that the Leonberger has twenty-two founder animals, or animal ancestors unrelated to one another (ten males and twelve females).

Things started to go wrong for the Leonberger even before World War II, however. For political reasons, the Nazi regime assigned a party official named Rudolf Schäfer,* who had written the breed standards for other dogs, to rewrite the Leonberger breed standard. Schäfer was not very familiar with Leonbergers, so his 1938 breed standard did not correspond well with the way Leonbergers actually looked and behaved, and it deviated significantly from the breed standard that Albert Kull had created. In 1951, another Deutsche Club für Leonberger Hunde rewrote the breed standard again, making it essentially identical to Stadelmann's 1924 prewar breed standard. Finally, things were back on track.

In 1963, one Robert Beutelspacher was appointed to the position of Zuchtbuchführer (breed registrar) at the DCLH. He soon became an influential figure in the Leonberger community, and his efforts to collect and report breeding data made him famous among dog aficionados. He initiated a Leonberger studbook (an official record of Leonberger pedigrees) that encompassed all of Europe, and with the DCLH president, Dr. Hermann Herbstreith, a veterinarian, he revised the breed standard yet again and developed various breeding

---

* Bliss-Isberg, *Leonberger*, 316.

Fun Leonberger Facts

- The Leonberger was recognized by the American Kennel Club in 2010 as its 167th breed.[*]
- The Leonberger is unique in the AKC for being the only dog in the Working Group originally bred to be a companion.[†]
- According to an estimate prepared by BioMed Central, there were around 30,000 Leonbergers in the world in 2020.[‡]
- There are around 3,300 Leonbergers in North America—2,300 in the United States and 1,000 in Canada.[§]
- The five countries with the most Leonbergers, in order, are France, with nearly 8,000; Germany, with more than 4,000; and Great Britain, the United States, and Sweden, with approximately 2,300 each.[¶]
- The country with the highest number of Leonbergers per capita is Finland, with nearly 2,000 Leonbergers among a population of 5.5 million people.[**]

---

[*] AKC Communications, "AKC Welcomes the Cane Corso, Icelandic Sheepdog and Leonberger," June 30, 2010, https://www.akc.org/press-releases/akc-welcomes-the-cane-corso-icelandic-sheepdog-and-leonberger/.

[†] AKC staff, "Meet 31 Purposely-Bred Dogs," August 1, 2020, https://www.akc.org/expert-advice/lifestyle/working-group-dogs/.

[‡] Anna Letko et al., "Genomic Diversity and Population Structure of the Leonberger Dog Breed," *Genetics Selection Evolution* 52, no. 61 (October 2020), https://gsejournal.biomedcentral.com/articles/10.1186/s12711-020-00581-3.

[§] Sharon Springel, "Understanding Mean Kinship," *LeoLetter*, October 2018, 60.

[¶] "Springel, "Understanding Mean Kinship."

[**] "Springel, "Understanding Mean Kinship."

rules and regulations. In 1974, Dr. Herbstreith passed away, and Beutelspacher became the president of the DCLH.* At that point their DCLH breed standard of 1972 became the official FCI breed standard.† Dr. Herbstreith's breeding regulations thus became enforceable, and in 1978 the International Leonberger Clubhouse in Leonberg was constructed.‡ In addition, in 1975, the German Leonberger club brought all Leonberger clubs together and formed the Internationale Union für Leonberger Hunde.§

Leonbergers have a long history in North America and the United States—despite the fact that until 1985, there were only seventeen Leonbergers known to be living in the United States.¶

In the 1870s, Leonbergers were brought to Newfoundland to invigorate the stock of Newfoundland dogs. Around the same time, two Leonbergers named Caesar and Sultan were purchased from Essig's kennel and transported across the ocean to join the Wellesley-Sterling theater company in the United States as the stars of their productions.** Then in 1879, Caesar and Sultan visited President Ulysses S. Grant, who called them the largest and most magnificent dogs he had ever seen and presented them with gold medals.†† During the years between World War I and World War II, a New Jersey family, the Wolfs, opened their home as a temporary refuge for Jews fleeing

---

* Believe it or not, Robert Beutelspacher was also a mailman, and he had to deal with attacking dogs in his line of work. So he helped advertise a spray that harmlessly deterred attacking dogs. See Bliss-Isberg, *Leonberger*, 130.
† Bliss-Isberg, *Leonberger*, 319.
‡ Bliss-Isberg, *Leonberger*, 131–32.
§ Also known as the Leonberger Union or the International Union for Leonberger Dogs, at https://www.leonbergerunion.com/.
¶ Lusby, *Leonberger*, 15.
** Bliss-Isberg, *Leonberger*, 60.
†† Bliss-Isberg, *Leonberger*, 64.

Germany: they also imported Leonbergers.* Unfortunately, this introduction of the breed into the United States did not last, and it would be another fifty years before the Leonberger appeared in America again.

During the late 1970s and the 1980s, a few families—Waltraut and Klaus Zieher, Brian Peters, Manfred and Sylvia Kaufmann, Keri Campbell and Melanie Brown, and Mary and Reiner Decher—brought Leonbergers to the United States. The Dechers had started a breeding program and were looking for a mate for their first dam, Viona.† By chance their neighbor discovered through a newsletter that there was another Leonberger in the United States, and that led to the families' finding and connecting with one another. I should add that the Dechers were careful to conform to the German breeding regulations and performed hip X-rays that they then submitted to the Orthopedic Foundation for Animals (OFA). Viona became the first OFA-certified Leonberger in America.‡

On Saturday, November 2, 1985, eight of these Leonberger enthusiasts met at a hotel in Denver, Colorado, to found the Leonberger Club of America (LCA). This group of founders, which has since been dubbed the Denver Eight,§ appointed a registrar, formulated a breeding acceptability checklist, and instituted various policies, including the requirement that OFA certification is mandatory for breeding. LCA membership grew: it held social gatherings, began publishing *LeoLetter*, and imported an increasing number of dogs. Now the LCA has thousands of members across the country, and Leonbergers receive high ratings on health tests relative to other large breeds. For example, in 2000, the OFA reported that only 14.6

---

* Bliss-Isberg, *Leonberger*, 101.
† Bliss-Isberg, *Leonberger*, 152.
‡ Bliss-Isberg, *Leonberger*, 152.
§ Bliss-Isberg, *Leonberger*, 154.

percent of Leonbergers tested positive for hip dysplasia, compared to 47 percent of Saint Bernards.[*]

Another important historical event was the founding of the Leonberger Health Foundation International (LHFI), in 2000 (it was just called the Leonberger Health Foundation back then). According to its website, the organization was founded by Waltraut Zieher and other members of the LCA's health, education, and research committee to "facilitate the solicitation and distribution of donations given to support health related breed-specific research." The LHFI also administers a program that collects DNA samples from Leonbergers to share with universities and research institutions, and of course it administers the Grey Muzzle Award.

LHFI's global biobank contains DNA samples from more than nine thousand Leonbergers. Among the organization's notable achievements are the eradication of Addison's disease among Leonbergers and the raising of nearly half a million dollars for research into conditions that affect canine health, including osteosarcoma, hemangiosarcoma, glaucoma, cardiac diseases, thyroid diseases, and neurological disorders. Its research also supports healthful longevity and aging as well as population diversity. Another success is the fact that since 2011, no Leonbergers with two copies of the LPN1 gene mutation (which causes Leonberger polyneuropathy) have been recorded in LHFI's biobank. LHFI is one of my favorite charities.

―

The end of the twentieth century marked not only the end of the Cold War but also the beginning of what I call the Dog Wars of America. In 1985, the American Kennel Club (AKC) registry comprised one-third of the world's known dog breeds. But the AKC had

---

[*] Bliss-Isberg, *Leonberger*, 176.

> **Leonbergers On-Screen**
>
> Did you know that three Leonberger dogs played the main character, Buck, in *The Call of the Wild: Dog of the Yukon* (1997)?[*] And that a Leonberger named Hagrid appeared on *Britain's Got More Talent* in 2017? Hagrid was attempting to set a new Guinness world record for catching the maximum number of sausages in his mouth in the shortest period of time.[†]
>
> [*] See Stuart Fitzgerald, "Leonberger," DogZone.com, at https://www.dogzone.com/breeds/leonberger/.
> [†] You can watch Hagrid's attempt at https://www.youtube.com/watch?v=eiLrHf-S8ck.

recognized only a few new breeds since 1887—a period of ninety-eight years. So the organization decided to change that policy, but this did not always go smoothly. The members of rare-breed clubs often did not want to be part of the AKC. For example, the Australian Shepherd Club of America (ASCA) was very reluctant to join, so a relatively small splinter group, the United States Australian Shepherd Association, was formed and designated the official member club of the AKC, which was not welcome news to the ASCA. The border collie is another example. Charles Krauthammer, the late political columnist, called the AKC the politburo of American dog breeding.[*]

Similarly, in 2003, a new Leonberger club was formed—the Leonberger Club of the United States—with the goal of becoming the Leonberger member club of the AKC. This essentially forced the LCA's hand, so they applied for membership in the AKC, a process

[*] Bliss-Isberg, *Leonberger*, 159.

that took years to complete. But ultimately the AKC approved the LCA as members in 2010: Leonbergers would officially become part of the Working Group. Fortunately, 90 percent of LCA breeders agreed to continue following LCA regulations regardless of whether the club would remain independent or become part of the AKC.* Also fortunately, AKC membership afforded more opportunities for Leonbergers to participate in dog shows, which is important to many owners.

---

* Bliss-Isberg, *Leonberger*, 187.

CHAPTER 12

Getting a Leonberger

Leonbergers are big and beautiful. They are loyal, loving, very social, playful, funny, intelligent, and eager to learn. They are amazing dogs with wonderful personalities. However, they also need a lot of exercise, brushing, attention, and space. They cannot be left unattended for long periods of time. These are things that you need to consider before getting a Leonberger.

When we got Bronco, our situation was fairly accommodating. Claudia was staying home with the kids, and she is good with dogs, having grown up with several of them. Our youngest child was eight years old. We have a spacious house with a fenced-in backyard, and we had time to exercise and socialize the puppy. If you live in a small apartment, if you are single, if both puppy parents work outside the home, or if you have very small children, then a Leonberger may not be the best choice for you.

In addition, if you think it's better to get two puppies so they can keep each other company while you're gone, you should think again. Leaving two puppies alone may be twice as bad as leaving one puppy alone—and if you're going to have to leave a puppy alone with any frequency, maybe your lifestyle isn't compatible with a Leonberger anyway.

So before Kennel von der Löwenhöhle would sell us the puppy, one of the owners asked us about our family and our living conditions. She sent us a form to fill out and asked us many questions.

To some people this practice may seem nosy, but it is not. The Leonberger community is very protective of its dogs and wants good homes for them. You won't find a Leonberger at Petland. If you're forced to return a dog to its breeder—or, much worse, if you return a dog to a shelter—that would be a great failure on your part and unfair to the dog. I should say that a reputable breeder will take back a dog rather than let you turn him in to a shelter. That's one reason why reputable breeders ask questions before they sell you a Leonberger. On pages 149–151 is the questionnaire Kennel von der Löwenhöhle sent us, along with Claudia's answers.

Sometimes, even if your circumstances are not ideal for getting a Leonberger, you can address specific issues before you get the dog. For example, I read about a young couple who owned a Leonberger and shared a house with other young couples. The others frequently forgot to lock the screen door, and therefore their Leonberger was often seen roaming the neighborhood unsupervised. Pressing buttons and handles is a piece of cake for a Leonberger. This was a dangerous situation. The solution? Certainly not a shock collar or an electronic fence. That's cruel and counterproductive.* The solution was to get the other people in the household to understand the gravity of the situation and cooperate.

Another thing to consider is cost. As of this writing, the price of a Leonberger is around $2,000 to $4,000 if you buy him from a

---

* George Hoppendale and Asia Moore, *Leonberger: Leonberger Dog Complete Owners Manual* (IMB Publishing, 2015), 83.

breeder—but that's merely the first expense. Your Leonberger will need a lot of care and supplies. There might also be unforeseen expenses, such as replacing an armchair that your Leonberger destroyed.

To make a rough estimate of your costs, figure that you'll need everything on the following list.

- Dry food
- Treats and dental chews
- Veterinary care, including vaccinations and prescription medications
- Professional training
- Monthly flea and tick medications
- Professional grooming
- Occasional dog-walking and/or dog-sitting services
- Microchipping
- Annual state and/or municipal registration
- Bowls
- Collars, leashes, and harnesses
- Beds
- Toys
- Gates and crates
- Brushes, nail clippers, and nail files
- Toothbrushes and toothpaste
- Shampoo and conditioner

Finding a Breeder

Let me say right away that you don't have to get your Leonberger from a breeder. You can also get him from a rescue organization, such as Leonberger Rescue Pals (LRPals.org). Puppy mills and pet stores should be avoided, but you're unlikely to find a Leonberger at those places anyway.

If you do get a puppy from a breeder, you should get him when he's between the ages of ten and sixteen weeks. No puppy should be removed from his mother and littermates before the age of eight weeks.[*] Make sure the breeder is registered with the Leonberger Club of America and ask for testimonials.[†]

Reputable breeders will most likely interview you to determine if you are a suitable Leonberger owner. As you would in a job interview, you should also ask questions of the breeders. Find out if they provide a return contract or other after-sale support. Ask the breeders what the emphasis and goals of their breeding programs are. If the answer is something along the lines of preserving the breed standard and improving the health of Leonbergers, you're off to a good start.

You can also ask for facts about a puppy's sire (father) and dam (mother), including their names, ages, temperaments, height, weight, and health. Ask if breeders can provide you with references from previous puppy buyers, veterinarians, or other breeders. Ask about the contract and what's in it. You could also ask breeders if they do temperament tests and what they do to help produce dogs who are obedient, nonaggressive, and confident. Ask about socialization, recommendations for food, and whether the dogs are raised to be kept in a kennel or in a house. Also ask if the puppy has received his vaccinations and deworming.

You may want to ask breeders if their puppies' parents, aunts, uncles, grandparents, and half siblings are clear of inherited diseases.

---

[*] Harriet Meyers, "What's the Best Age to Bring Your New Puppy Home?," American Kennel Club, February 19, 2021, at https://www.akc.org/expert-advice/puppy-information/best-age-bring-puppy-home/.

[†] The Leonberger Club of America can guide you when selecting a breeder. Visit their breeder list at https://leonbergerclubofamerica.com/leo-search/breeders.

The LCA requires breeders to test for hip dysplasia, elbow dysplasia, autoimmune thyroiditis, and Leonberger polyneuropathy. The CERF (Canine Eye Registration Foundation) eye examination is also required.

All LCA dogs used for breeding must have a CHIC (Canine Health Information Center) number. You can use the CHIC number of the puppy's parents to look up the results of their required tests.[*] If breeders dismiss your questions by telling you that their dogs don't have any health issues, they are most likely not being truthful. Perfection is unlikely, and breeders should be able to verify their claims.

If possible, visit the breeder you chose and pick out a puppy yourself. (We were not able to visit our Leonberger breeder, but as you know everything turned out great anyway.) Check to see if the puppy you're considering seems healthy. You may not want the most sluggish of the puppies, but you don't want the most energetic, either.

Preparing Your Home for a Leonberger

Before you bring your new puppy home, you should buy the following items and have them ready for use right away.

- Dry food
- Treats and dental chews
- Bowls
- Collars, leashes, and harnesses
- Beds
- Toys

---

* Go to http://www.caninehealthinfo.org/chicinfo.html and enter the number in the box that appears at the top right-hand corner of the page.

- Gates and crates
- Brushes, nail clippers, and nail files

Leonbergers have big, powerful jaws, and therefore the best food and water bowls are made of stainless steel or ceramic. These kinds of bowls are also easy to clean. Since your Leonberger will grow large fairly quickly, be sure to get large bowls. Your dog's water bowl should be filled with fresh water at all times.

Puppies, especially Leonberger puppies, love to chew on things, and that includes electrical cords and things that can get stuck in their throats. So install chew-safe cord covers in any area that's accessible to your dog.

It is recommended that you use a crate for house-training. (You might also want to use the crate for transportation.) The crate provides your puppy with his very own safe place—a place where he's reluctant to relieve himself. You should buy a wire crate large enough to hold a dog who is 31.5 inches tall at the shoulders. A wire crate will give him a full view of his surroundings and good ventilation. Wire is also difficult for him to chew through. Make sure to put a bowl of clean water in the crate with your dog.

Introduce your puppy to his collar as soon as he gets home, and let him get used to wearing it. There are many different kinds of collars to choose from. Lightweight nylon is a good choice for puppies. Make sure the collar is not too tight. You should be able to slip two fingers between his neck and the collar. Don't make it too loose, either. You don't want him slipping out of it while you're walking. Choke collars are not recommended for heavy-coated breeds such as Leonbergers because the chain can damage the long and abundant coat. For Bronco we used large nylon or leather collars most of the time.

An alternative to a collar is a harness, which you put on over the

Kennel von der Löwenhöhle Questionnaire

Why do you want a Leonberger?
We have a dog book, and while looking at dogs we came across the Leonberger, a gorgeous dog from Germany. We also had the opportunity to meet some Leonbergers, a mother and her puppies, which were wonderful. We have read that Leonbergers are great with children and good guard dogs, which is something we'd like. We have two dogs, but we have not raised them as puppies. We have never had a puppy and would like to have one.

What do you like about the Leonberger and what do you know about its characteristics? Do you prefer male or female? Why?
They are very beautiful and love to swim. We have a huge pool, and my children love to spend their summers swimming. Leonbergers also make wonderful pets and are good guard dogs, and best of all they don't drool. We don't prefer a male or a female dog.

Are you aware this is at least a ten-year commitment?
Yes. We have two other dogs, and of course we are aware that they live up to ten years—hopefully more.

Do you have any other pets? Have you had any experience raising a giant-breed puppy?
We have a Lab and a German shepherd. We have two dwarf hamsters, Moldova and Montenegro. My son also keeps a baby ball python in a cage in his room (UGGH). As I said before, we have never owned a puppy, but we met some Leonberger puppies from a breeder who resides in Houston.

Where will your dog be kept—indoors or outdoors? Backyard or kennel?
Our dog would be kept mostly indoors. (We live in Texas, and it would get too hot outside.) At night we take all our dogs for walks and for occasional swims during the year. When the dog is still a puppy, we would keep it in a puppy playpen and take it out every half hour to go to the bathroom (until obedience training). We do have a fenced backyard the puppy can play in, and we have a dog run with a dog door so the dogs can come and go as they please.

Is your yard fenced?
Yes. Our yard has a seven-foot-high solid wood fence all the way around.

How many hours will you be out of the house? Where will your Leonberger be while you are gone?
I am a stay-at-home mom, and we would almost always have someone in the house, such as our housekeeper, children, and family. If we are gone for a long periods of time, we have a dog sitter who comes to our house to take care of our dogs.

Do you have children? If so, what are their ages?
We have three kids, ages thirteen, ten, and eight. Two boys and one girl (in that order).

Describe a typical day at your house now. How do you think it will change once the puppy arrives?
On a typical day, the kids go to school, and I like to take a long walk. I go through some paperwork, I prepare dinner, then everyone comes home. On weekends, my younger kids have sports, but my oldest kid stays home (he plays during the week).

I would be with the dog most of the day and would do my shopping while the housekeeper is there. I do not plan on leaving the puppy for any long period of time. I'm sure that having the puppy will be like having another child. We have been told that the puppy will be quite rambunctious for the first three years of its life.

Have you observed any obedience classes in your area? It is very important that Leonberger puppies start obedience classes by sixteen weeks of age. Would you attend such classes?
We have not observed any obedience classes yet. However, we are interested in the International K9 training facility in Dallas and would absolutely attend these classes.

Von der Löwenhöhle puppies start their crate training at our kennel. Will you continue this training? If not, why not?
Yes, we would continue crate training at our home. We will follow your advice and that of our veterinarians in regard to further training.

What plans do you have for your Leonberger—e.g., showing, breeding, obedience, family companion, therapy? If you plan to show or breed, what experience, if any, have you had?
Our major purpose for wanting a Leonberger is to have a family companion.

Please add any other information you feel will help us pick out a puppy for you.
We would like a dog that will fit in well with our family.

dog's shoulders and around his torso. One advantage of a harness is that it can be attached to a car seat belt.

There are many types of leashes, too, including those made of nylon, cotton, and leather. You can buy chain leashes, retractable leashes, and elastic leashes. Retractable leashes seem very attractive because you can allow your dog to explore without having to run after him. However, they're not that easy to handle when quick action is needed or if your dog is not obeying your commands.

All puppies chew, especially during the three-to-five-month teething period, when the adult teeth are breaking through the gums. Chew toys are a great way to redirect this chewing energy. Puppies especially love to chew on soft woolly toys. There are chew toys that squeak and chew toys that quack—just make sure they don't have button eyes or noses that your puppy can swallow. Also, be careful with rawhide. You don't want fragments of these things ending up in your dog's stomach.

You also don't want your dog chewing on your shoes or those of your visitors—unless the shoes belong to someone you'd rather not have in your home. (On the other hand, without shoes, visitors can't leave.) It is difficult for dogs to distinguish between shoes they're permitted to chew and shoes they're not permitted to chew. So it's not a good idea to give puppies old shoes as chew toys.

Socialization

The first twenty weeks of a Leonberger puppy's life are the most important. During this time, he needs to socialize with people and other dogs, which will allow him to grow into a stable and confident adult. One of the most important early socialization experiences your puppy will have is his first visit to the veterinarian, and that should happen very soon after you've brought him home.

Leonbergers are very social dogs, naturally friendly and unafraid, and they love being around people and other dogs. Not every breed is this easy to socialize, but even with a Leonberger, you still need to work on it. (Keep in mind that your puppy should have received his first and second rounds of vaccinations before you socialize him with other dogs.)

Since Leonbergers love being around people, it's best if someone is at home with your dog during the day. It is important that Leonbergers feel like part of the family and that they aren't left alone for hours on end.

It is also important that you keep a consistent schedule. Meals, walks, bedtime, and other events should take place the same time each day. And a behavior that's forbidden on one day shouldn't be permitted on the next.

Leonbergers are big dogs and need a lot of exercise. An adult Leonberger should get at least one hour—ideally, two and a half hours—of exercise per day. That could be in the form of walking, running, swimming, or playing. However, puppies shouldn't be taken for long walks. When they are younger than three months old, they are likely to get enough exercise just by playing around the house. Young puppies can easily get injured, too, so don't allow them to climb stairs or play roughly with older dogs.

The All-Important Coat

Leonbergers are double-coated.* They have a soft pale undercoat and a coarse topcoat as well as a lot of hair around the ears, neck, and legs. Leonbergers will shed twice a year, and during those periods the

---

* Madeline Lusby, *Leonberger: A Comprehensive Owner's Guide* (Allenhurst, NJ: Kennel Club Books, 2005), 72.

> **Leader of the Pack**
>
> Dogs are pack animals, and one of the first things they need to do when they arrive in your home is identify the leader of the pack—or family. In our case, when Bronco was a puppy, that was Claudia, because she was the one who was at home with him and took care of him for most of the day. Later on, after I retired and as Bronco got older, this changed, because I became his primary caregiver.
>
> Any puppy or adult dog will anoint the person who feeds him and stays with him the most as the alpha person. This is the person your dog will try to please and obey. It is important that the alpha person is not the dog himself. (Although whenever someone called me and asked to speak to the head of the household, I gave the phone to Bronco.) Show your dog that you're the leader by being confident and calm. It also helps to touch his food and leave your scent on it while you're preparing to feed him.

undercoat will fall away. Note that "twice a year" doesn't mean one Tuesday morning in March and one Friday afternoon in September: it means two extended periods of the year. In fact, hair will fall off Leonbergers pretty much all year. You will need to brush your dog's coat frequently, preferably every day.

Brushing a Leonberger is not a trivial matter. You'll need a slicker brush, a rubber brush, a dematting rake, and perhaps a bristle brush.[*] First, go over the entire coat gently with a slicker brush, smoothing

---

[*] Michael Stonewood, *The Leonberger: A Complete and Comprehensive Owners Guide to Buying, Owning, Health, Grooming, Training, Obedience, Understanding, and Caring for Your Leonberger* (self-pub., 2019), 49.

out the tangles. Then use the dematting rake to remove mats, then use the rubber brush to remove dead hair and give the dog a massage. The bristle brush can be used at any time to keep the dog's hair shiny and clean.

Claudia took care of most of Bronco's brushing when he was young, but as he got older, we didn't brush him as often as we needed to, and we had issues with knots and mats. Because of a misunderstanding with a groomer, our request for removing a few knots and mats led to Bronco's being shaved all over. Claudia was quite upset when she picked him up after his appointment. Shaving the coat off a Leonberger is not recommended (that's an understatement). Among other things, a Leonberger's coat keeps him cool in the heat and protects

Bronco gets an outdoor bath.

> ## Caring for an Aging Leonberger
>
> Bronco was technically a senior for more than half his life. He lived a long time, and he was healthy overall, but during his last couple of years, age took a toll on him. It's important that you know that the end of your dog's life is coming and prepare yourself for it. Returning a dog because you can't handle him in old age is a huge failure on your part. Unfortunately, many senior dogs end up in shelters, and they typically have to wait longer than other dogs to be adopted. Often, they're euthanized.* This should not happen, but it does. People who love the puppy but don't want to deal with the old dog he inevitably turns into should not get a puppy in the first place.
>
> Old dogs will often have health problems, including hearing loss, loss of eyesight, incontinence, and various illnesses that get worse as time passes. But despite all the difficulties, caring for an old dog can be one of the most rewarding experiences in life. For me, it was an experience that was profound—both emotionally and, in a sense, spiritually. I made a connection with another living being with whom I could not speak and
>
> * "Senior Dogs: Caring for Them in Their Golden Years," Top Dog Foundation, October 31, 2017, at https://topdogfoundation.org/senior-dogs-caring-for-them-in-their-golden-years/.

him from the sun year-round. Fortunately, Bronco's coat grew back—for the most part—but it was a bad experience, especially for him. That was a lesson we learned the hard way. It should also be noted that trimming or altering the coat of a Leonberger will disqualify you from showing him in competition. Show dogs need to have their natural coats.

yet could understand as he was approaching the end of his life.

One thing to be aware of is that a dog who has been housetrained for years will feel shame if he is not able to go outside to relieve himself. Your reaction should not be anger but understanding and kindness. To help your dog, take him out more often, and if that is not enough, just get used to cheerfully cleaning up the mess without complaints.

Old dogs may also show signs of cognitive decline, just as humans do. Toward the end of his life, Bronco occasionally wandered about aimlessly in the middle of the night and appeared restless. Sometimes he was just thirsty and wanted to get to his water bowl, but at other times he didn't seem to know what he was doing. When this happened, I just followed him around and tried to comfort him. He would soon return to his bed, where he wanted to be petted and fall back asleep.

An old dog needs more frequent veterinary checkups than a young dog does. Avoid rough play, and don't allow children and rambunctious puppies to bother him. Old dogs still love to go for walks, but take it slow and stop to rest more frequently and for longer periods of time. Allow your old Leonberger the pleasure of walking in moderation.

Old dogs need high-quality low-grain food that's relatively

Leonbergers shouldn't be bathed frequently. Bathing them a few times a year is sufficient. You'll need a large tub, basin, or kiddie pool. (You could also just use your own bathtub or shower if it has enough room for your dog.) Don't use human shampoo on a dog, because it's too harsh for his coat and not good for his skin. Massage dog shampoo into the fur, making sure to keep it away from the eyes, low in calories. Most national dog food brands sell senior versions of their products. In addition, as Bronco got older and had a hard time getting up on our sofas, we realized that the floor was not comfortable for him anymore. So we bought him large soft dog beds that we placed in his favorite spots around the house.

Another issue to watch for is arthritis. If your dog is limping, is favoring a limb, or seems to have stiff or sore joints, take him to the veterinarian for a diagnosis. Arthritis is often detectable on an X-ray. There are also over-the-counter medications to help relieve the pain and swelling.[*] Our veterinarian prescribed a joint supplement called Dasuquin that works together with glucosamine and chondroitin to protect cartilage.[†]

If your dog has arthritis, it is even more important than usual to keep his weight down and his nails trimmed. If your dog makes a clickety-clack sound when he walks on hard surfaces, his nails aren't short enough.

[*] Kathy Davieds, "Vet Advice: Relieving Your Dog's Arthritis," *The Bark*, May 2011, at https://thebark.com/content/vet-advice-relieving-your-dogs-arthritis.
[†] India Arnold, "How to Care for an Aging Dog," *PetHelpful*, March 15, 2021, at https://pethelpful.com/dogs/Caring-for-an-Aging-Dog-Tricks-Your-Old-Dog-Needs-You-to-Learn.

then rinse thoroughly. Afterward, dry your dog with a towel. If you use a hair dryer, don't put it on the hottest setting.

Pouring water on a Leonberger to cool him off on a hot summer day might be ineffective because of his water-resistant double coat. In fact, it could make matters worse, because the water makes the hair stick together, which could block the vaporization that cools the skin. Instead, pour water on your Leonberger's paws, head, and belly near the back legs, where the coat is thinner. I admit I was pouring water on Bronco to cool him for years before I discovered that it's a bad idea. If your house isn't air-conditioned, you can buy a cooling mat, but make sure that your dog doesn't chew it. Cooling-mat material is often dangerous to ingest.

CHAPTER 13

Leonberger Health

Scientific veterinary research has shown that large dogs have a much shorter life span than small dogs. This is not controversial, yet so many people are surprised by it. For example, one day after Bronco had just visited the veterinarian and I was walking him around the shopping center, a woman came up to me and asked about him. I told her he was twelve—old for a Leonberger. She said, "Twelve isn't very old; my Chihuahua lived to be sixteen." I explained to her that big dogs, especially really big dogs such as Leonbergers and Saint Bernards, don't live as long as small dogs do, so for a Leonberger, Bronco was indeed really old. The look on her face told me she didn't believe me; excuses, excuses, excuses. So this fact is far from intuitive to people, especially considering that big animals tend to live longer than small animals in the wild.

The cliché that one human year corresponds to seven dog years is a myth.* For example, the average life span of a Great Dane is eight

---

* Randa Kriss, "Dog Age Chart: How Old Is Your Dog in Human Years?," *Prrrs&Wags*, August 21, 2020, at https://www.pumpkin.care/blog/dog-age-chart/.

to ten years. For a Chihuahua, it is twelve to twenty years. Dachshunds and Pomeranians live between twelve and sixteen years, and pugs live between twelve and fifteen years. The average life span of a Leonberger, by contrast, is eight to nine years (some sources say seven years[*]). You can look up your dog's particulars online: the product-review website Goody Pet features a life-expectancy calculator for hundreds of dog breeds.[†]

Knowing the expected life span of your dog has value. When a dog reaches three-quarters of it, for example, he is considered a senior and needs to be treated differently.[‡] You should get dog food that's especially made for senior dogs and visit the veterinarian more often—ideally, twice a year.

To take Bronco's temperature, we used a thermometer that we could insert into his ear canal. However, you can also do it the old-fashioned way: coat a thermometer with petroleum jelly or baby oil and gently insert it about one inch into your dog's anus. Wait sixty seconds, then remove the thermometer. It should be noted, however, that the old-fashioned approach may lead to protests.

It's also important to keep careful track of your Leonberger's weight. Obesity in dogs is a growing problem: according to the Association for Pet Obesity Prevention, in 2018, 56 percent of American dogs were obese.[§] Obesity, by definition, is a condition in which a person—or an animal—weighs at least 30 percent more than his ideal weight. In the photo on page 24, in which Bronco is sitting on Claudia's lap, he weighed 167 pounds—thirty-two pounds above his

---

[*] The American Kennel Club is one of these sources: https://www.akc.org/dog-breeds/leonberger/.
[†] See https://www.thegoodypet.com/dog-life-expectancy-calculator.
[‡] See Madeline Lusby, *Leonberger: A Comprehensive Owner's Guide* (Allenhurst, NJ: Kennel Club Books, 2005), 115.
[§] See https://petobesityprevention.org/.

ideal weight of 135 pounds. Soon after that photograph was taken, we put him on a diet. Obesity can cause a lot of health problems, including diabetes, heart disease, early-onset arthritis, and joint pain. It can also put a strain on the body's vital organs.

Reasons to Visit a Veterinarian

- Body temperature below ninety-nine degrees or above 104 degrees[*]
- Refusing food for twenty-four hours
- Diarrhea or vomiting lasting longer than twenty-four hours
- Blood in the stool
- Unexplained weight loss or gain
- A drastic change in eating or drinking habits
- Excessive salivation
- A lump in the throat; several lumps or bumps on or under the skin as well as other places
- Ingestion of toxins
- Loss of elasticity in the skin
- Lethargy
- Signs of pain (panting, licking lips, crying, avoiding touch, flinching)
- Trouble chewing or swallowing
- Lameness
- Signs of bloat (see page 164)

[*] A dog's normal body temperature is between 100.5 and 102.5 degrees Fahrenheit, compared to between ninety-seven and ninety-nine degrees Fahrenheit for humans. See Lusby, *Leonberger*, 111.

Inherited and Partially Inherited Conditions

Leonbergers, especially those bred in North America, are fortunate compared to other large breeds. The Leonberger breed standard (see page 183) does not call for traits that can be detrimental to health, and the Leonberger community, especially the LHFI, has been successful in eliminating or reducing inherited conditions. Recent advances in canine genetics and medical technology have given breeders new tools for breeding healthy dogs.

In addition, Leonbergers benefit from the existence of several health registries and databases. Examples include the OFA's Canine Eye Registration Foundation (CERF), Companion Animal Eye Registry (CAER), and Canine Health Information Center (CHIC) (see pages 147 and 202). There is also the Worldwide Independent Leonberger Database (see page 192). When breeders use the available tools and certify their dogs, it makes a big difference.

Following is a list of some inherited and partially inherited conditions that can occur in Leonbergers.

Addison's Disease

Addison's disease, an autoimmune condition, is characterized by low adrenal gland function, which negatively affects metabolism. The symptoms include weakness, vomiting, diarrhea, dehydration, increased thirst, and loss of appetite. These symptoms are common in many illnesses, which makes Addison's disease difficult to diagnose in its early stages. Severe symptoms include hair loss, low temperature, dehydration, and shaking. Not all cases of Addison's disease are inherited: it can also be caused by tumors, for example. However, an inherited form of Addison's disease suddenly showed up in the early 1990s among Leonbergers. Fortunately, LHFI-supported researchers were able to determine a genetic pattern of inheritance—a nonpenetrant recessive trait. Through careful breeding, Addison's disease was virtually eliminated in Leonbergers.

Bloat

Another condition affecting large, deep-chested dogs is bloat, or gastric dilatation and volvulus. This occurs when a dog's stomach expands (gastric dilatation) because of food, fluid, or gas, thus putting pressure on other organs and causing dangerous problems, including restriction of blood flow to the heart and stomach lining, a tear in the wall of the stomach, and breathing difficulties. In some cases, the stomach will twist or rotate (volvulus).

The causes of bloat are not entirely known, but suspected risk factors include having one large meal per day, eating or drinking too fast or too much, eating from a raised bowl,* and strenuous exercise after eating. For this reason, it is recommended that Leonbergers eat at least twice a day. There may be a genetic component, too: if any of your dog's relatives has had the condition, your dog might be more susceptible to it.

If your dog gets bloat, it is important that you get him help right away. Symptoms include restlessness, drooling, anxiety, pacing, a swollen stomach, and dry heaves. He might also stretch with his front end down and rear end up. If the condition gets worse, he may suffer weakness, shortness of breath, and rapid heartbeat. Eventually he may collapse. Bloat is potentially fatal, so if you suspect your dog has it, get him to a veterinarian or an emergency clinic immediately. Find out where your nearest twenty-four-hour veterinary facility is and keep the information handy. For dogs who have already suffered bloat, and perhaps for large deep-chested dogs in general, it might be

---

* Patrick Wardell, "Raised Feeders = Bloat Risk?," Visionary Keto Pet Foods, September 10, 2019, at https://visionarypet.com/blogs/keto-news/raised-feeders-bloat-risk.

worth considering stomach tacking, or gastropexy, in order to avoid bloat in the future.*

Cancer

Cancer is the most common killer of purebred dogs: in fact, nearly half of them die from some form of cancer.† Overall, the most common form is skin cancer. In Leonbergers, bone cancer and hemangiosarcoma are the most common forms. As in humans, early detection can save or extend the life of your dog. Warning signs of cancer include

- weight loss,
- bleeding or discharge from a body cavity,
- bumps or lumps that keep growing,
- persistent stiffness or lameness,
- breathing difficulties,
- bad breath or bodily odors,
- difficulty with defecation or urination,
- difficulty with eating or swallowing,
- lesions that won't heal,
- sores that recur or won't heal, and
- loss of appetite.

Naturally, not every one of these signs and symptoms is applicable to all types of cancer. The only sign of Bronco's squamous cell carcinoma was a lesion that wouldn't heal. Also see the sections on hemangiosarcoma and osteosarcoma below.

---

* Catherine Barnette, "Gastropexy," VCA Hospitals, at https://vcahospitals.com/know-your-pet/gastropexy.
† Lusby, *Leonberger*, 116.

Dilated Cardiomyopathy

Dilated cardiomyopathy (DCM) is a disease of the heart muscle that causes the left ventricle to enlarge and cease functioning correctly. Arrhythmias can develop, which can be life-threatening. Your dog may faint, lose weight, cough, exhibit shortness of breath, or retain fluid.

Elbow Dysplasia

Elbow dysplasia is caused by malformation or degeneration of the elbow joint and is very common in large dog breeds. The symptoms are pain and limping and can start when your dog is only four months old. It is diagnosed via X-rays and regulated by the OFA, just as hip dysplasia is.[*]

Hemangiosarcoma

Hemangiosarcoma (HSA) is an aggressive cancer of the blood vessels. It often appears as a mass in the spleen, liver, or heart but can also be found elsewhere. It is challenging to diagnose and equally difficult to treat. It is most common in golden retrievers, German shepherds, and Labrador retrievers but can occur in Leonbergers as well. In addition to genetic factors, certain toxins are associated with this cancer. Fortunately, there is a promising blood test (called the Shine On Study, or SOS) that identifies features of rare cells linked to this cancer and a novel drug therapy called eBAT (EGF bispecific ligand targeted angiotoxin). Both SOS and eBAT are still in the clinical-study phase at the time of this writing, but they offer hope for early detection and treatment.[†]

---

[*] "Small Elbow Dysplasia," American College of Veterinary Surgeons, at https://www.acvs.org/small-animal/canine-elbow-dysplasia.

[†] Sharon M. Albright, "Researching New Treatments for Canine Hemangiosarcoma," American Kennel Club Canine Health Foundation, June 5, 2020, at

Hip Dysplasia

Hip dysplasia is a common and devastating problem in large purebred dogs. A dog with hip dysplasia has an incorrectly formed hip joint in his hind leg. As the years pass and the joint keeps being used, it wears abnormally, becoming increasingly loose, and the joints may become arthritic. Sometimes hip dysplasia may manifest itself much earlier, even before the age of one. The Leonberger Club of America decreed that member kennels are only allowed to breed dogs who are certified as free of hip dysplasia for three generations. As a result, hip dysplasia is rare in Leonbergers.

Hypothyroidism

Hypothyroidism is caused by an underactive thyroid gland, which in turn causes other bodily functions to slow down. Symptoms include lethargy, weight gain, excessive hunger, and hair and skin changes.

Laryngeal Paralysis Polyneuropathy

Laryngeal paralysis and polyneuropathy are actually two separate conditions that often occur together. Laryngeal paralysis is characterized by a change in bark and, sometimes, noisy or difficult breathing. Polyneuropathy is characterized by a worsening gait, exercise intolerance, and weakness in the hind legs as a result of degradation of the nerve fibers.

Bronco appeared to have suffered from geriatric-onset laryngeal paralysis polyneuropathy, or GOLPP, although he was never given an official diagnosis. By the time he showed signs of the condition, he was also suffering from heart failure, and making a definitive

---

https://www.akcchf.org/educational-resources/library/articles/researching-new-treatments.html.

diagnosis would have required general anesthesia, which we didn't want to subject him to.

However, after Bronco died, we asked the doctors to take a blood sample and skin sample, as suggested by LHFI, because his DNA was needed for longevity research. We were also interested in finding out if he carried any defective genes that could have caused GOLPP.

We submitted the samples to researchers at the University of Minnesota, who are supported by LHFI. They tested for the presence of four defective genes—LEMP, LPN1, LPN2, and LPPN3. As it turned out, Bronco was clear with respect to all four.[*]

Leukoencephalomyelopathy

Canine leukoencephalomyelopathy (LEMP) is characterized by slowly worsening gait abnormalities, especially spontaneous knuckling, dragging of the paws, and incoordination of the forelegs. It can be diagnosed with an MRI.[†] The disease is caused by a genetic mutation: a Leonberger with two copies of the LEMP gene mutation, denoted LEMP-D/D, is referred to as affected/susceptible and will often develop the disease. A Leonberger with only one defective gene, denoted LEMP-D/N, will not get the disease, but he is a carrier. If two carrier dogs mate, their offspring can get the disease. A clear dog (as Bronco was) has no copies of the LEMP mutation, and he is denoted LEMP-N/N.

---

[*] For information about the genetic likelihood of a dog carrying the genes that cause GOLPP, see the report published by researchers at the University of Bern and the University of Zurich in October of 2020: https://www.genetics.unibe.ch/unibe/portal/fak_vetmedizin/c_dept_dcr-vph/h_inst_genetics/content/e20974/e85824/e95237/e102197/LPN_EN_Interpretation_2020Oct31_eng.pdf.

[†] "Leukoencephalomyelopathy," University of Minnesota College of Veterinary Medicine, at https://vetmed.umn.edu/research/labs/canine-genetics-lab/genetic-research/leonberger-leukoencephalomyelopathy.

Osteochondritis Dissecans

Osteochondritis dissecans (OCD) is an abnormal development of cartilage in certain joints. It can lead to arthritis and appears to have environmental as well as genetic causes.

Osteosarcoma

Osteosarcoma is an aggressive type of bone cancer that tends to spread to the lungs. It affects both young and old dogs and, like osteochondritis dissecans, appears to have environmental as well as genetic components. But according to the American Kennel Club,

---

Canine Genetics

The thirty thousand Leonbergers[*] alive in the world today are all descended from a small number of dogs. As a result, Leonbergers tend to have a high coefficient of inbreeding (COI), or the probability that an individual with two identical genes received both genes from a single ancestor.[†] But Bronco had a relatively low ten-generation COI of 8.76 percent.

Of course all purebred dogs are more or less inbred, which comes with inherent health risks. However, the precise and restrictive breeding regulations of the Leonberger Club of America and other Leonberger clubs, and the work of the LHFI, have resulted in Leonbergers being relatively free of

[*] See Anna Letko et al., "Genomic Diversity and Population Structure of the Leonberger Dog Breed," *Genetics Selection Evolution* 52 (October 2020), at https://gsejournal.biomedcentral.com/articles/10.1186/s12711-020-00581-3.
[†] For a detailed explanation of coefficient of inbreeding, see the one offered by the Worldwide Independent Leonberger Database at http://www.leonberger-database.com/coi_e.html.

inherited illnesses compared to other large dog breeds in America.*

In addition, modern veterinary care for dogs has become quite advanced: indeed, a lot of veterinary knowledge and procedures are derived from medicine for humans. One fact that most people are unaware of is that there is an equivalent dog gene for 75 percent of human genes,[†] which certainly helps. Another fact that may surprise some people is that scientists have demonstrated that all purebred dogs have at least four "genetic time bombs" embedded in their genotype.[‡]

The canine genome was sequenced in 2004,[§] and new detrimental mutations are continually identified. It seems like removing carrier dogs (dogs with defective genes who are not necessarily afflicted themselves) from the breeding pool would be a good idea. However, the LHFI does not recommend this, because, for example, 14 percent of all Leonbergers are carriers of the LEMP mutation.[¶] In short, removing carrier dogs for this and other conditions wouldn't leave much to breed with.

---

* Humane Society Veterinary Medical Association, "Guide to Congenital and Heritable Disorders in Dogs," rev. 2011, at https://www.hsvma.org/assets/pdfs/guide-to-congenital-and-heritable-disorders.pdf.
† Centre for Agriculture and Bioscience International, "Dog and Man Share 75% of DNA," September 26, 2003, at https://www.cabi.org/agbiotechnet/news/3177.
‡ Caroline Bliss-Isberg, *Leonberger: A Comprehensive Guide to the Lion King of Breeds* (Sea Cliff, NY: Revodana Publishing, 2017), 377.
§ National Human Genome Research Institute, "Dog Genome Assembled," National Institutes of Health, July 14, 2004, at https://www.genome.gov/12511476/2004-advisory-dog-genome-assembled.
¶ Per the report published by the University of Bern and the University of Zurich: https://www.genetics.unibe.ch/unibe/portal/fak_vetmedizin/c_dept_dcr-vph/h_inst_genetics/content/e20974/e85824/e95237/e804309/LEMP_EN_Interpretation_2020Oct31_eng.pdf.

> If you want to submit a DNA sample from your Leonberger for research purposes, go to the website of the University of Minnesota College of Veterinary Medicine at https://z.umn.edu/leonberger for instructions. You can also go to the website of the University of Bern, in Switzerland, for information and instructions: https://www.genetics.unibe.ch/services/dog/gene_tests_in_the_leonberger/index_eng.html.

research into the disease in dogs is likely to have benefits for children who suffer from it as well.[*]

Infectious Diseases

Another threat to your dog's health is infectious disease. You can avoid many infectious diseases by preventing your dog from ingesting rotten food or contaminated water, including the water in communal water bowls, and by avoiding putting your dog in a situation where he could be bitten by another animal. Fortunately, there are many vaccinations available today, too. A list of common infectious diseases follows.

Coronavirus

Here I'm not speaking of the SARS-CoV-2 virus that causes COVID-19 in humans but enteric canine coronavirus (CCoV) and respiratory canine coronavirus (CRCoV). There are hundreds of coronaviruses, seven of which are known to infect humans. Signs of coronavirus

---

[*] See Stephanie Gibeault, "Bone Cancer Genome in Dogs Could Help Decipher Disease in Children," American Kennel Club, November 4, 2019, at https://www.akc.org/expert-advice/health/bone-cancer-in-dogs-may-help-treat-disease-in-kids/.

infection, which is extremely contagious, include diarrhea and vomiting.*

Distemper

Distemper is a highly contagious virus that can turn fatal in dogs very quickly. The symptoms include a yellow-green ocular discharge followed by coughing, nasal discharge, vomiting, and reduced appetite.

Hepatitis

Canine hepatitis, or canine adenovirus 1, begins in the tonsils and after four to eight days spreads into the bloodstream and internal organs, especially the liver. The symptoms include tonsillitis, fever, vomiting, diarrhea, swollen lymph nodes, an enlarged liver, abdominal pain, and, in severe cases, coagulation disorder, the collapse of blood vessels, and death.

Kennel Cough

Kennel cough, also known as bordetella, is a highly contagious respiratory disease caused by a combination of bacteria and a virus. Symptoms include a persistent dry cough, retching, and a watery nasal discharge. In severe cases it can lead to pneumonia and even death. Young puppies and old dogs are most severely affected.

Leptospirosis

Leptospirosis is a potentially fatal bacterial infection that spreads through the bloodstream and can lead to kidney and liver failure. Symptoms include rapid dehydration, increased urination, sore muscles, shivering, lack of appetite, diarrhea, and vomiting, possibly with

---

* Rania Gollakner and Ernest Ward, "Canine Coronavirus Disease," VCA Animal Hospitals, at https://vcahospitals.com/know-your-pet/coronavirus-disease-in-dogs.

blood. It can also cause difficulty breathing, spontaneous cough, and dark red-speckled gums.

Lyme Disease

Borrelia burgdorferi is a tick-borne bacterium that causes Lyme disease, which is characterized by fever, lameness, and lack of appetite.

Ticks are arachnids that may, in the larva stage, appear as small dark specks on your dog's fur. Nymphs and adults are larger. An unfed adult is as big as an apple seed and is flat in appearance.

Ticks feed on the blood of their hosts. In the process, they can transmit not only Lyme disease but other infectious agents as well. Ticks have even been shown to play a role in certain cancers, including hemangiosarcoma and lymphosarcoma. There are several places where you can send ticks for analysis to see if they harbor Lyme disease or other infectious agents.[*]

If you discover a tick on your dog, you can remove it with tweezers or your fingers, if they're covered in plastic wrap or plastic gloves. The tick should be grasped as closely as possible to the dog's skin and pulled straight upward. After pulling the tick out, disinfect the site of attachment using chlorhexidine or an iodine solution. Do not use rubbing alcohol or hydrogen peroxide on dogs.

Parvovirus

Parvovirus is a potentially fatal and highly contagious disease. An affected dog will become lethargic a few days after infection, then he will suffer from severe vomiting and diarrhea. Parvovirus is a disease that primarily affects puppies: for this reason, puppies should not go to dog parks until they have had all their puppy shots.

---

[*] "Tick Submission and Testing," Texas Department of State Health Services, August 13, 2021, at https://www.dshs.texas.gov/idcu/health/zoonosis/tickBites/.

Rabies

Rabies is a well-known and potentially deadly disease that is primarily spread by animal bites. It can kill humans as well as dogs. Symptoms in dogs include fever, difficulty swallowing, excessive drooling, staggering, seizures, behavior changes, foaming at the mouth, aggression, and even paralysis. However, once your dog is showing symptoms, it is usually too late. So if your dog gets bitten by an animal, take him to the veterinarian immediately. Rabies is 100 percent preventable with vaccination.[*]

Parasites

Parasite control typically begins when your dog is two weeks old. He should start on heartworm-prevention medication when he's no older than eight weeks. And I certainly recommend using one of the many methods of preventing flea and tick infestation, including topical medications, that are readily available today.

Still, avoiding all parasites throughout a dog's life is difficult. Mosquitoes in particular carry all sorts of parasites that infect dogs. Following is a list of some of the most common offenders.

Fleas

Did you hear about the dog who went to a flea circus and stole the show? But seriously, folks . . . flea infestation is a fairly common problem for dogs. The most frequent symptom is itching. However, some dogs are allergic to fleas and can have more severe symptoms, such as scabs and hair loss. In addition, fleas can transmit tapeworms to dogs. There are many ways to prevent flea infestation, including maintaining a clean house, shampooing your carpets, going over your dog's

---

[*] "Rabies in Dogs," *Fetch*, at https://pets.webmd.com/dogs/rabies-dogs#1.

coat with a flea comb, bathing your dog, and applying over-the-counter flea-prevention products monthly throughout the year.

Giardiasis

Giardiasis is a common canine intestinal infection caused by the protozoan parasite giardia. It is also common in humans—the usual symptom is diarrhea—and can be treated with medication and bath-

---

Canine Vaccinations

Rabies vaccination is required in all fifty states; several other vaccines may also be required, depending on where you live. But even if they're optional, I suggest that you consult with your veterinarian about which of the vaccines listed below you should give your dog—and give him booster shots whenever your veterinarian recommends them.

- Adenovirus: Because there are undesirable side effects associated with the vaccine that contains adenovirus 1, most hepatitis vaccines now contain adenovirus 2 instead. Fortunately, this is effective as well.
- Bordetella: This vaccine is often administered through a nasal spray but can also be given as an injection or oral drops.
- Borreliosis: This is not a core vaccine but it is recommended if you live in an area where your dog is at risk for Lyme disease.
- Coronavirus: This vaccine provides protection against the enteric canine coronavirus (CCoV) but not the respiratory canine coronavirus (CRCoV).

> - Distemper (DHPP): This is a core vaccine that prevents distemper, parvovirus, parainfluenza, and two types of adenovirus (hepatitis). Dogs should receive the DHPP vaccine at eight, twelve, and sixteen weeks of age, then again one year later, and then one to three years after that.
> - Leptospirosis: Even though this vaccine is not 100 percent effective, most veterinarians still recommend it.
> - Rabies: Vaccinating dogs against rabies will prevent its spread not only among dogs but also among humans.
> - Other vaccines include those for the canine flu as well as "lifestyle vaccines," such as those for dogs who live in an area that puts them at high risk of being bitten by rattlesnakes (for example).

ing. Dogs often get the parasite by ingesting the feces of infected animals.

Heartworm

Heartworm disease is caused by a roundworm, *Dirofilaria immitis*. The usual symptoms are cough, exercise intolerance, fatigue, and weight loss. Eventually, the disease can lead to heart failure and, sometimes, death. Heartworms are transmitted by infected mosquitos that are found across most of the United States. Therefore, preventive heartworm medications should be given as directed by your veterinarian. The American Heartworm Society features an incidence map on its website that can help you discover how prevalent heartworm disease is in your area: https://www.heartwormsociety.org/pet-owner-resources/incidence-maps.

Hookworm

Hookworms are intestinal worms that are approximately two to three millimeters (an eighth of an inch) in length. They ingest large amounts of blood from the blood vessels in the intestinal wall, which can cause anemia. If your dog has enough of them, they can cause inflammation in the intestine. Hookworms sometimes cause diarrhea in adult dogs, but puppies tend to get sicker and may experience vomiting, diarrhea, weight loss, pale gums, and weakness. Hookworms are also zoonotic, meaning that they may infect humans. Preventive heartworm medications often prevent hookworms as well.

Mites

Skin diseases caused by mites are referred to as mange. The two most common mites found in dogs are Demodex and Sarcoptes. Demodex mites are not contagious and are found naturally on a dog's skin. An overgrowth of Demodex mites is thought to be related to a compromised immune system in adult dogs or underdeveloped immune systems in puppies. Sarcoptes, on the other hand, is contagious—even to humans—and causes sarcoptic mange in dogs, characterized by intense itching. The good news is that there are many effective treatments for sarcoptic mange.

Neosporosis

Neosporosis is an infection caused by the *Neospora caninum* parasite. In puppies, symptoms include stiffness of the hind legs, paralysis as a result of gradual muscle atrophy, and rigid contraction of the limbs. In older dogs, symptoms include seizures, tremors, behavioral changes, blindness, and, sometimes, difficulty swallowing.

Canine CPR and the Heimlich Maneuver

If you see signs that your dog's heart may have stopped—for example, if he doesn't move, his chest is still, you can't feel his breath, you can't hear or feel his heartbeat, his gums and lips are gray, his pupils are dilated, and you can't find a pulse—your dog may need CPR. But keep in mind that CPR is potentially hazardous and can cause serious damage if performed on a healthy dog. CPR should only be performed when necessary. If possible, call a veterinarian and have him or her help you over the phone.

The following instructions are taken from the American Red Cross and PetMD.com.*

First, check for a pulse by placing your index fingers near the inside top of your dog's hind leg and try to feel a heartbeat. You can also try to detect the heartbeat in the chest.

If you feel no pulse, find a flat spot and lay the dog on his side—either side is fine. Stand or kneel beside the dog.

Place one of your palms on the dog's rib cage, over the heart region, and put your other palm on top of it.

Without bending your elbows, press the rib cage down about one-quarter to one-third of the way, then let go. Do this at a speed of around 100–120 compressions per minute. Many veterinarians do chest compressions to the beat of the song "Stayin' Alive," the 1970s disco hit. It sets the appropriate pace.

After around thirty compressions, close the dog's mouth tightly and breathe into his nose twice. If there are two people

---

* See https://www.redcross.org/take-a-class/cpr/performing-cpr/pet-cpr; http://www.vetstreet.com/dr-marty-becker/check-your-dogs-vital-signs-at-home; https://www.petmd.com/dog/emergency/common-emergencies/e_dg_cardiopulmonary_resuscitation; https://www.petmd.com/dog/emergency/common-emergencies/e_dg_choking.

present, one of you can do the breathing through the dog's nose and the other can do the chest compressions.

Continue performing the compressions and rescue breaths until the dog begins to breathe and a heartbeat returns. Check for a pulse once per minute.

Naturally, get the dog to a veterinarian as soon as possible.

If the dog has a pulse but doesn't breathe, his airway may be blocked.

In that case, perform the Heimlich maneuver. If the dog is lying down on his side, place one hand on his back for support and use the other hand to squeeze the abdomen upward and forward toward the spine. If the dog is conscious and standing, put your arms around his belly, joining your hands. Make a fist and push firmly up and forward, just behind the rib cage. Place the dog on his side afterward. Check his mouth for any dislodged objects. If you can see the object, hold his jaws open, grasp it, and pull.

But if your Leonberger is conscious and choking, he may be pawing at his mouth and panicking. This makes it very difficult to hold his jaws open and reach your hand inside his mouth, considering that his bite has a force of 399 PSI. In that situation, you must use your best judgment.

Roundworm

Most puppies are born with Ascaris roundworms, which they inherit from their mothers. It is recommended that you take a stool sample from your puppy prior to his first veterinary exam. This is not a dangerous worm, but you still want to get rid of it, not least because it could be transmitted to humans. It easily treated with deworming medication.

Tapeworm

Tapeworms are fairly long, up to eight inches, and can exist in a dog's intestines without causing many symptoms. Dogs get tapeworms by ingesting fleas infested with tapeworm larvae or by eating infested rabbits, rodents, or reptiles. This is also easily treated with deworming medication.

ACKNOWLEDGMENTS

First and foremost, I would like to thank my wife, Claudia, for the extraordinary love and commitment she showed in caring for Bronco throughout his lifetime. She provided many of the stories in this book, and she read and fact-checked the manuscript carefully. Because of her, I was able to remember and honor Bronco with the truthfulness he deserves.

I would also like to thank our children—Jacob, David, and Rachel—for helping us care for Bronco and the other dogs they grew up with. Our children, all adults now, also contributed several of their memories for this book.

Many thanks are due to Claudia's parents, Jack and Etty Sardas, for the exceptional help, love, and support they have devoted and continue to devote to our entire family, including Bronco and our other dogs, and for contributing additional stories that made their way into these pages.

Many thanks as well to Claudia's sisters—Dora, Marianne, and Isabella—and our niece Jessica, all of whom helped us with Bronco at various points in his life.

Julie Schaffert, our breeder, deserves a huge thank-you—not only for selling us Bronco but also for helping us during his first year with paperwork, advice, and instructions. We are grateful that she kept in touch with us and that she allowed me to reprint the questionnaire on pages 149–151.

I also would like to thank the Leonberger Club of America and all their volunteers for their efforts to keep America's Leonbergers healthy and safe. Thanks, too, to the Leonberger Health Foundation International and the Worldwide Independent Leonberger Database for everything their volunteers do to keep the Leonberger breed strong and for providing useful information to all Leonberger owners and breeders free of charge.

In addition, I would like to thank the Preston Royal Animal Clinic, in Dallas, for their loving and professional care and for keeping Bronco and our other dogs in tiptop shape.

Finally, I would like to thank my editor, Barbara Clark, for her diligence with every sentence and paragraph in this book; our illustrator, Naomi Rosenblatt, for her lovely drawings, which accurately depict and thus greatly enhance the stories; Eileen Chetti, our proofreader, whose eagle eye is second to none; Susan Hood, our book designer, who put it all together beautifully; and consultants Dean Burrell and the late and much missed Robin Lynn Brooks, who helped me get Bronco's story into print and out into the world.

APPENDIX 1
THE LEONBERGER BREED STANDARD

There is more than one breed standard for Leonberger dogs. The worldwide breed standard was published by the Fédération Cynologique Internationale (FCI) in 2002: FCI standard number 145.[*] The photograph on page 190 summarizes its key points. The American Kennel Club (AKC) has published a similar document that now serves as the official breed standard of the Leonberger Club of America.[†]

Leonbergers are large muscular double-coated dogs. The height of an adult male is between 28 and 31.5 inches (72 to 80 centimeters) at the withers. The height of an adult female is between 25 and 29.5 inches (65 to 75 centimeters) at the withers. (The withers is the ridge located between the shoulder blades of an animal, on the back right below the neck.) Reputable breeders try to maintain these characteristics.

---

[*] You can view and download the standard at http://www.fci.be/Nomenclature/Standards/145g02-en.pdf.

[†] The American Kennel Club standard is found at https://images.akc.org/pdf/breeds/standards/Leonberger.pdf.

Leonbergers are sexually dimorphic—that is, there are noticeable differences between males and females. This is not always the case in dogs. Female Leonbergers are usually smaller and look more feminine.[*]

Males typically weigh between 120 and 170 pounds, and females usually weigh between 100 and 135 pounds. For comparison's sake, below are the standard heights and weights for male dogs of other breeds.

- An Irish wolfhound, the world's tallest dog (when standing on two feet), is 32 inches tall at the withers and weighs between 120 and 155 pounds.
- A Great Dane stands between 31 and 35 inches at the withers and weighs between 110 and 180 pounds.
- A Saint Bernard is between 28 and 35 inches tall at the withers and weighs between 140 and 180 pounds.
- A German shepherd stands between 24 and 26 inches at the withers and weighs between 66 and 86 pounds.

In other words, the Leonberger is right there among the largest breeds in the world.

Your Leonberger must closely match the breed standard if you are planning to show him or breed him. Minor deviations from the standard are generally tolerated in shows, but disqualifying faults are not tolerated. Sometimes Leonberger puppies who significantly deviate from the breed standard cannot be shown and can't be used for breeding. But they are still Leonbergers, and they are still wonderful and worthy of all our love and respect.

---

[*] See Rebecca O'Connell, "9 Impressive Facts About the Leonberger," *Mental Floss*, February 22, 2016, at https://www.mentalfloss.com/article/75615/9-impressive-facts-about-leonberger.

Following is the official FCI breed standard for Leonbergers.

General Appearance

According to his original purpose, the Leonberger is a large, strong, muscular, elegant dog. He is distinguished by his balanced build and confident calmness, yet he has quite a lively temperament. Males, in particular, are powerful and strong.

Important Proportions

Height at the withers to the length of the body: 9 to 10. The depth of the chest is nearly 50 percent of the height at the withers.

Behavior/Temperament

As a family dog, the Leonberger is an agreeable partner for present-day homes and living conditions who can be taken anywhere without difficulty and is distinguished by his marked friendliness toward children. He is neither shy nor aggressive. As a companion, he is agreeable, obedient, and fearless in all situations of life.

The following are particular requirements of a steady temperament:

- Self-assurance and superior composure
- Medium temperament (including playfulness)
- Willingness to be submissive
- Good capacity for learning and remembering
- Insensitivity to noise

Head

On the whole, the head should be deeper than it is broad and elongated rather than stocky. The proportion of the length of the muzzle to the length of the skull should be about 1 to 1. The skin should fit closely all over without any wrinkles.

CRANIAL REGION

Skull: In profile and seen from the front, slightly arched. In balance with the body and limbs, it is strong but not heavy. The skull at its back part is not substantially broader than it is near the eyes.

Stop: Clearly recognizable but moderately defined.

FACIAL REGION

Nose: Black.

Muzzle: Rather long, never running to a point; nasal bridge of even breadth, never dipped, rather slightly arched (Roman nose).

Lips: Close-fitting, black, corners of lips closed.

Jaws/Teeth: Strong jaws with a perfect, regular, and complete scissor bite, the upper teeth closely overlapping the lower teeth without any gap, and teeth set square to the jaw with 42 sound teeth according to the dentition formula (missing M3 tolerated). Pincer bite is accepted; no constriction at the canines in the lower jaw.

Cheeks: Only slightly developed.

Eyes: Light brown to as dark brown as possible, medium size, oval, neither deep-set nor protruding, neither too close together nor too wide apart. Eyelids close-fitting, not showing any conjunctiva. The white of the eye (the visible part of the sclera) not reddened.

EARS

Set on high and not far back, pendant, of medium size, hanging close to the head, fleshy.

Neck

Running in a slight curve without break to the withers. Somewhat long rather than stocky, without throatiness or dewlap.

Body

WITHERS
Pronounced, especially in males.

BACK
Firm, straight, broad.

LOINS
Broad, strong, well muscled.

CROUP
Broad, relatively long, gently rounded, flowing to merge with tail set on; never overbuilt.

CHEST
Broad, deep, reaching at least to the level of the elbows. Not too barrel-shaped; more oval.

UNDERLINE AND BELLY
Only slightly tucked up.

Tail

Very well furnished; while standing, it hangs down straight; also, in movement, it is only slightly curved, and if at all possible, it should not be carried above the prolongation of the topline.

Limbs

Very strong, especially in males.

FOREQUARTERS

General appearance: Forelegs straight, parallel, and not too close.

Shoulders / Upper arms: Long, sloping, forming a not-too-blunt angle; well muscled.

Elbows: Close to the body.

Pastern: Strong, firm; seen from the front, straight; seen from the side, almost vertical.

Forefeet: Straight (turning neither in nor out), rounded, tight, toes well arched; black pads.

HINDQUARTERS

General appearance: Seen from the rear, position of the hind legs not too close; parallel.

Hocks and feet: Turned neither in nor out.

Pelvis: Slanting.

Upper thigh: Rather long, slanting, strongly muscled. Upper and lower thigh form a distinct angle.

Hocks: Strong, distinct angle between lower thigh and rear pastern.

Hind feet: Standing straight, only slightly longish. Toes arched; pads black.

Gait/Movement

Ground-covering, even movement in all gaits. Extending well in front with good drive from the hindquarters. Seen from front and behind, the limbs move in a straight line when walking or trotting.

Coat

HAIR

Medium soft to coarse, profusely long, close-fitting, never parted, with the shape of the whole body visible despite the thick undercoat. Straight or slight wave still permitted; forming a mane on neck and chest, especially in males; distinct feathering on front legs and ample breeches on hind legs.

COLOR

Lion yellow, red, reddish brown; also sandy (pale yellow, cream-colored) and all combinations in between, always with a black mask. Black hair tips are permitted; however, black must not determine the dog's basic color. Lightening of the basic color on the underside of the tail, the mane, the feathering on the front legs, and the breeches on the hind legs must not be so pronounced as to interfere with the harmony of the main color. A small white patch or stripe on the chest and white hairs on the toes are tolerated.

Height at the Withers

Dogs: 72 to 80 centimeters (recommended average 76 centimeters).
Bitches: 65 to 75 centimeters (recommended average 70 centimeters).

Faults

Any departure from the foregoing points should be considered a fault, and the seriousness with which the fault should be regarded should be in exact proportion to its degree and its effect upon the health and welfare of the dog.

Disqualifying Faults

- Aggressive or overly shy dogs.
- Any dog clearly showing physical or behavioral abnormalities.
- Severe anatomical faults (i.e., pronounced cow hocks, pronounced roach back, bad swayback; front feet turning out extremely). Totally insufficient angulation of shoulder, elbow, stifle, or hock joints.
- Brown nose leather.
- Very strong lack of pigment in lips.
- Absence of teeth (with the exception of M3). Overshot, undershot, or other faults in mouth.
- Eyes without any brown.
- Entropion, ectropion.

From the Féderation Cynologique Internationale breed standard

Head: On the whole deeper than broad and elongated rather than stocky.
Stop: Clearly recognizable but moderately defined.
Eyes: Light brown to as dark brown as possible, medium size, oval.
Nose: Black
Muzzle: Rather long, never running to a point.
Lips: Close fitting, black, corners of lips closed.
Jaws/Teeth: Strong jaws with a perfect, regular and complete scissor bite.
Chest: Broad deep, reaching at least to the level of the elbows.
Forequarters: Forelegs straight and not too close. Shoulders/Upper arm long, sloping, well muscled. Elbows are close to the body. Pastern is strong and firm. Forefeet straight (not turning in or out), rounded, tight, toes well arched, black pads.

Ears: Set on high and not far back, pendant, of medium size, hanging close to the head, fleshy.
Neck: Running in a slight curve without break to the withers.
Back: Firm, straight, broad.
Underline and belly: Only slightly tucked up.
Hair: Medium soft to coarse, profusely long, close fitting, never parted, with the shape of the whole body visible despite the thick undercoat.

Croup: Broad, relatively long, gently rounded.
Color: Lion yellow, red, reddish brown, also sandy (pale yellow, cream colored) and all combinations in between, always with a black mask.
Tail: Very well furnished. While standing, it hangs down straight.
Hindquarters: Pelvis slanting. Upper thigh long, slanting. strongly muscled. Upper and lower thigh form a distinct angle. Hocks strong, distinct angle between lower thigh and rear pastern. Hind feet when standing straight only slightly longish. Toes arched, pads black.

Appendix 1: The Leonberger Breed Standard

- Distinct ring tail or too highly curled-up tail.
- Brown pads.
- Cords or strong curls.
- Faulty colors (brown with brown nose and brown pads; black and tan; black; silver; wild-coat color).
- Complete lack of mask.
- Too much white (reaching from toes onto pasterns); white on chest larger than palm of hand, white in other places).

N.B.

- Male animals should have two apparently normal testicles fully descended into the scrotum.
- Only functionally and clinically healthy dogs, with breed-typical conformation, should be used for breeding.

APPENDIX 2
THE WORLDWIDE INDEPENDENT LEONBERGER DATABASE

The Worldwide Independent Leonberger Database* is a very large and nearly complete database that contains information about more than 160,000 Leonbergers who lived as far back as the late nineteenth century. Considering that there are thirty thousand living Leonbergers in the world, that is quite impressive. The database is updated weekly and free to use. It serves mostly as a tool for breeders and researchers, but it is quite interesting for anyone to browse. It was established in 2005 as a nonprofit organization and is managed and owned by Wilma and Ben Kroon, breeders who live in the Netherlands.

For each Leonberger, the database contains the following information.

- Full name
- A photograph if available

---

* The database, which is still growing, can be found at http://www.leonberger-database.com.

Appendix 2: The Leonberger Database

- Registration number
- Tattoo and/or microchip number
- DNA profile number
- Date and place of birth
- Kennel name
- Website of breeder
- Website of owner
- Export registration number
- Mean kinship (a measure of genetic diversity)
- Indicators of hip dysplasia (abbreviated as HD) and elbow dysplasia (abbreviated as ED)
- Eye test dates and results*
- Indicators of hypothyroidism
- Results of DNA tests for the genes LPN1, LPN2, LPPN3, and LEMP
- Number of offspring
- Coefficient of inbreeding for ten generations and all generations

Like any database, it is fully searchable. Search criteria include the name (or portion of a name), registration number, date of birth, and chip number. You can search in English, German, and French. The website also features informative articles about the data that's collected. Note that some of Bronco's information is missing because he was not used for breeding.

With the help of the database, I was able to trace Bronco's lineage all the way back to 1901, and I found photographs of and other information about several of his ancestors as far back as 1904.

I also found out that twenty-one Leonbergers were born on the

---

* Conditions tested for include cataracts, distichiasis, ectropion, glaucoma, goniodysgenesis, macroblepharon, and persistent pupillary membranes (abbreviated PPM).

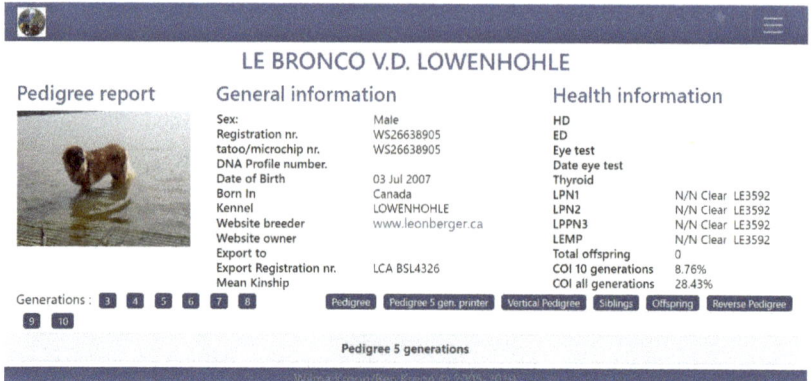

This screen shot shows the information about Bronco that appears in the WILD database above his full pedigree.

same day as Bronco, five of them in Canada. Before I searched, I didn't know the names of Bronco's siblings, but now I do. And I found out that thirty-one Leonbergers out of the more than 160,000 in the database had or have the name Bronco. Three of them were born in North America.

APPENDIX 3
LEONBERGER QUIZ

Try this quiz on your friends and family—the answers appear on page 197.

1. *Which of the following features makes the Leonberger an excellent swimmer?*
    A) Huge lung capacity
    B) Webbed paws
    C) Gills located behind the ears

2. *How big is an adult male Leonberger?*
    A) 29–31 inches tall at the withers and 100–150 pounds
    B) 28–31.5 inches tall at the withers and 120–170 pounds
    C) 30–34 inches tall at the withers and 140–190 pounds

3. *According to the breed standard, what is the proper color for a Leonberger's mask?*
    A) Black
    B) Brown
    C) Yellow or tawny

4. Which of the following foods is safe for Leonbergers to eat?
   A) Onions
   B) Chocolate
   C) Cooked chicken breast

5. The first Leonberger was registered in what year?
   A) 1846
   B) 1930
   C) 1959

6. Who registered the first Leonberger?
   A) Otto von Bismarck
   B) Princess Marie of Romania
   C) Heinrich Essig

7. Legend has it that the Leonberger was bred for which purpose?
   A) To resemble a cross between a lion and a wolf
   B) To resemble the lion in the town crest of Leonberg
   C) To be the biggest dog in the world

8. What is a Leonberger's average life expectancy?
   A) Six to seven years
   B) Eight to nine years
   C) Ten years

9. Leonbergers were used for what purpose in World War I?
   A) To pull ammunition carts
   B) To comfort wounded soldiers
   C) To detect land mines

10. According to BioMed Central, approximately how many Leonbergers were there worldwide in 2020?
    A) 14,000

Appendix 3: Leonberger Quiz

    B) 23,000
    C) 30,000

11. **When was the Leonberger Club of America founded?**
    A) 1886
    B) 1921
    C) 1985

12. **Which disease that showed up among Leonbergers in 1990s was largely eliminated?**
    A) Addison's disease
    B). Laryngeal paralysis polyneuropathy
    C) Parvovirus

13. **The Leonberger Health Foundation International gives an award to long-lived Leonbergers. How old does a Leonberger have to be to qualify?**
    A) Eight
    B) Ten
    C) Twelve

14. **In what year was the Leonberger recognized by the American Kennel Club?**
    A) 1963
    B) 2010
    C) 2020

15. **The Leonberger is thought to be a combination of which three breeds?**
    A) Saint Bernard, Landseer Newfoundland, and Pyrenean mountain dog
    B) Great Dane, Saint Bernard, and Irish wolfhound
    C) Newfoundland, Great Dane, and Bernese mountain dog

Answers

1. B
2. B
3. A
4. C
5. A
6. C
7. B
8. B
9. A
10. C
11. C
12. A
13. C
14. B
15. A

RESOURCES AND REFERENCES

Books

Bliss-Isberg, Caroline. *Leonberger: A Comprehensive Guide to the Lion King of Breeds.* Sea Cliff, NY: Revodana Publishing, 2017.

Hoppendale, George, and Asia Moore. *Leonberger: Leonberger Dog Complete Owners Manual.* N.p.: IMB Publishing, 2015.

Lusby, Madeline. *Leonberger: A Comprehensive Owner's Guide.* Allenhurst, NJ: Kennel Club Books, 2005.

Stonewood, Michael. *The Leonberger: A Complete and Comprehensive Owners Guide to Buying, Owning, Health, Grooming, Training, Obedience, Understanding, and Caring for Your Leonberger.* Self-pub., 2019.

Online Resources

Leonberger Organizations

International Union for Leonberger Dogs: https://www.leonbergerunion.com/
Leonberger Club of America: https://www.leonbergerclubofamerica.com/.
Leonberger Health Foundation International: https://www.lhfi.org/
Worldwide Independent Leonberger Database: http://www.leonberger-database.com.

Breed Overviews

American Kennel Club: https://www.akc.org/dog-breeds/leonberger/.
Dog Zone: https://www.dogzone.com/breeds/leonberger/.
Mental Floss: https://www.mentalfloss.com/article/75615/9-impressive-facts-about-leonberger.
Nationwide Insurance: https://www.petinsurance.com/healthzone/pet-breeds/dog-breeds/leonberger/.

Breed Histories

Kennel Ex Horto Leonis: https://www.leonbergerunion.com/breed-history.html.
Leonberger Union: https://leonbergerunion.com/history.htm.

Breed Standards

American Kennel Club: https://images.akc.org/pdf/breeds/standards/Leonberger.pdf.
Fédération Cynologique Internationale: http://www.fci.be/Nomenclature/Standards/145g02-en.pdf.
German Kennel Club (in German): https://www.vdh.de/welpen/mein-welpe/leonberger.

Genetics

Centre for Agriculture and Bioscience International: https://www.cabi.org/agbiotechnet/news/3177.
Genetics Selection Evolution: https://gsejournal.biomedcentral.com/articles/10.1186/s12711-020-00581-3.
Humane Society Veterinary Medical Association: https://www.hsvma.org/assets/pdfs/guide-to-congenital-and-heritable-disorders.pdf.
National Human Genome Research Institute: https://www.genome.gov/12511476/2004-advisory-dog-genome-assembled.
University of Bern, LEMP: https://www.genetics.unibe.ch/unibe/portal/fak_vetmedizin/c_dept_dcr-vph/h_inst_genetics/content/e20974/e85824/e95237/e804309/LEMP_EN_Interpretation_2020Oct31_eng.pdf.
University of Bern, LNP1: https://www.genetics.unibe.ch/unibe/portal/fak

_vetmedizin/c_dept_dcr-vph/h_inst_genetics/content/e20974/e85824/ e95237/e102197/LPN_EN_Interpretation_2020Oct31_eng.pdf.

Medical Conditions

Bloat: https://pets.webmd.com/dogs/gastric-volvulus-bloat-dogs.

Bloat: https://www.petmd.com/dog/conditions/digestive/signs-and-symptoms-bloat-dogs.

Coronavirus: https://www.petmd.com/dog/conditions/digestive/c_dg_canine_coronavirus_infection.

CPR: https://www.redcross.org/take-a-class/cpr/performing-cpr/pet-cpr.

CPR: https://www.petmd.com/dog/emergency/common-emergencies/e_dg_cardiopulmonary_resuscitation.

Dilated cardiomyopathy: https://www.petmd.com/dog/conditions/cardiovascular/c_dg_cardiomyopathy_dilated.

Distemper: https://www.petmd.com/dog/conditions/respiratory/c_dg_canine_distemper.

Geriatric onset laryngeal paralysis polyneuropathy: https://www.pethealthnetwork.com/dog-health/dog-surgery-a-z/geriatric-onset-laryngeal-paralysis-polyneuropathy-golpp.

Heartworm: https://www.heartwormsociety.org/pet-owner-resources/incidence-maps.

Heatstroke: https://www.vets-now.com/pet-care-advice/heatstroke-in-dogs/.

Heimlich maneuver: https://www.petmd.com/dog/emergency/common-emergencies/e_dg_choking.

Hemangiosarcoma: https://www.petmd.com/blogs/fullyvetted/2012/july/hemangiosarcoma_in_dogs-26511.

Hemangiosarcoma: https://www.akcchf.org/educational-resources/library/articles/researching-new-treatments.html.

Hepatitis: https://www.petmd.com/dog/conditions/infectious-parasitic/c_dg_canine_hepatitis.

Hip dysplasia: https://www.akc.org/expert-advice/health/hip-dysplasia-in-dogs/.

Hookworms: https://www.petmd.com/dog/conditions/infectious-parasitic/c_multi_ancylostomiasis.

Kennel cough: https://www.petmd.com/dog/conditions/respiratory/c_dg_canine_tracheobronchitis.

Leptospirosis: https://www.petmd.com/dog/conditions/infectious-parasitic/c_multi_leptospirosis.

Lyme disease: https://www.petmd.com/dog/conditions/infectious-parasitic/c_dg_lyme_disease.

Mites: https://www.petmd.com/dog/conditions/skin/c_dg_sarcoptic_mange.

Neosporosis: https://www.petmd.com/dog/conditions/infectious-parasitic/c_dg_neosporosis.

Obesity: https://petobesityprevention.org/.

Osteochondritis dissecans: https://www.petmd.com/dog/conditions/musculoskeletal/c_dg_osteochondrosis.

Osteosarcoma: https://www.petmd.com/dog/conditions/musculoskeletal/c_multi_osteosarcoma.

Osteosarcoma: https://www.akc.org/expert-advice/health/bone-cancer-in-dogs-may-help-treat-disease-in-kids/.

Parvovirus: https://www.petmd.com/dog/conditions/infectious-parasitic/c_dg_canine_parvovirus_infection.

Rabies: https://www.petmd.com/dog/conditions/neurological/c_multi_rabies.

Squamous cell carcinoma: https://www.petmd.com/dog/conditions/cancer/c_dg_squamous_cell_carcinoma_skin.

Ticks: https://www.petmd.com/dog/conditions/infectious-parasitic/c_multi_ticks.

Miscellaneous

Adoption: http://www.petfinder.com/.

Bringing a puppy home: https://www.akc.org/expert-advice/puppy-information/best-age-bring-puppy-home/.

Canine Health Information Center Certification Program: https://www.ofa.org/about/chic-program#chicinfo.html.

Eye drops: https://www.youtube.com/watch?v=MikAmnSl1uM.

Grey Muzzle Award: https://www.leohealth.org/grey-muzzle-hall-of-honor.html; https://youtu.be/qS9w6Zk1Hz4.

"Heel" command: https://www.sfspca.org/sites/default/files/dog_commands_heel.pdf.

Resources and References

Life expectancy: https://www.thegoodypet.com/dog-life-expectancy-calculator.
Memorial site for dogs: https://www.rainbowsbridge.com/.
National Dog Registry: http://www.nationaldogregistry.com/.
Orthopedic Foundation for Animals: https://www.ofa.org.
Pet travel: http://www.pettravel.com/.
Poisonous plants: https://poisonousplants.ansci.cornell.edu/dogs/index.html.
Ten tips for a poison-safe household: https://poisonousplants.ansci.cornell.edu/dogs/ten_tips.html.

www.ingramcontent.com/pod-product-compliance
Lightning Source LLC
Chambersburg PA
CBHW051545010526
44118CB00022B/2588